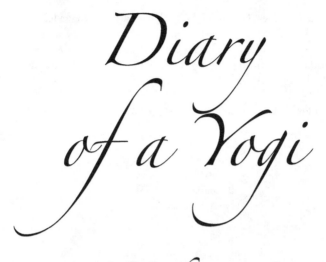

Diary of a Yogi

A Book of Awakening

GUAN SHI YIN

Copyright © 2018 Guan Shi Yin.

All rights reserved. No part of this book may be used or reproduced by any means, graphic, electronic, or mechanical, including photocopying, recording, taping or by any information storage retrieval system without the written permission of the author except in the case of brief quotations embodied in critical articles and reviews.

Balboa Press books may be ordered through booksellers or by contacting:

Balboa Press
A Division of Hay House
1663 Liberty Drive
Bloomington, IN 47403
www.balboapress.com
1 (877) 407-4847

Because of the dynamic nature of the Internet, any web addresses or links contained in this book may have changed since publication and may no longer be valid. The views expressed in this work are solely those of the author and do not necessarily reflect the views of the publisher, and the publisher hereby disclaims any responsibility for them.

The author of this book does not dispense medical advice or prescribe the use of any technique as a form of treatment for physical, emotional, or medical problems without the advice of a physician, either directly or indirectly. The intent of the author is only to offer information of a general nature to help you in your quest for emotional and spiritual well-being. In the event you use any of the information in this book for yourself, which is your constitutional right, the author and the publisher assume no responsibility for your actions.

Any people depicted in stock imagery provided by Getty Images are models, and such images are being used for illustrative purposes only. Certain stock imagery © Getty Images.

Print information available on the last page.

ISBN: 978-1-9822-1230-8 (sc)
ISBN: 978-1-9822-1229-2 (hc)
ISBN: 978-1-9822-1239-1 (e)

Library of Congress Control Number: 2018911084

Balboa Press rev. date: 09/14/2018

Contents

Acclaim for 'Diary of A Yogi' vii
Quotes ix
Dedication xi
Acknowledgments xiii
Preface xv
Foreword xvii
Fact xix
Introduction xxi
About Guan Shi Yin xxiii
About Altair Shyam xxv

Chapter 1   Samye 1
Chapter 2   Zahor 9
Chapter 3   Eden 25
Chapter 4   Koya-san 37
Chapter 5   Kailash 49
Chapter 6   Ketumati 60
Chapter 7   On the Road to Sarnath 76
Chapter 8   Pleiades 87
Chapter 9   Potalaka 103
Chapter 10 Kalachakra 121
Chapter 11 Avalon 130
Chapter 12 Shambhala 2425 142

Epilogue 151
Free Extract from 'Diary of A Yogi Guide –
    Portals of Presence' 153
Portals of Presence – Samye – Dream Yoga 157
Practice 165

Acclaim for 'Diary of A Yogi'

I have known Stephen for two decades. I call him a friend, but really he's so much more than that. One time, years ago, I was in Japan and my life was unravelling. Stephen asked me to meet him at a Shinto shrine. From there, he took me deep into a nearby forest. I didn't emerge from that forest for about eight hours. There, seated on the forest floor, I met Altair Shyam and he pieced me back together. His wisdom, his knowledge, his ability to access energy, his capacity to gently reach into you and reveal your potential is utterly unique. I left that forest a different person and gave Stephen the nickname, Forest Yoda.

I have been fortunate to meet many healers and teachers on my travels, but only one Forest Yoda. Stephen's gifts are incomparable and include the talent for weaving wisdom into tales. He has always been a wonderful storyteller, no doubt a legacy of his Maori heritage. But for years I've been telling him to write his story, *the story*... the story that will help others.

This is it. *Diary of a Yogi - A TRUE STORY* is more than a book. It is a journey you take that will profoundly impact your life. This is your chance to go into the forest with Stephen and emerge transformed.

Jane Tara
www.janetara.com

"This book is a treasure, wrapped in a gift, enclosed in a temple. It resonates with the essence of the human spirit in all of us. Allow it to flow, unfold and bloom in your heart — you will be rewarded with ecstasy (standing outside oneself)."

Marty F
Seattle, WA

"Thank you for giving me one of the greatest gifts ever.

Tears just came flowing through my eyes from the start of the reading to the end. Not tears of sadness though but tears of relief, of hope, of validation, of redemption, of grace, of liberation, of joy, of gratitude, of renewal.

Oh wow! Someone sees all my visions too!

Thank you for answering the call to uplift me from the mirage. May I honor your service by being in service to all, God, Divine Mother, bring into my consciousness.

A.M.D.G. ('Ad Majorem Dei Gloriam' – all for the greater glory of God)

Love and Infinite Blessings,

Yan A
Haiti

PS If one of my visions of having a house near the ocean come true, you have the first invitation to come and stay for as long as you want and with your loved ones too."

Quotes

"To be fully alive, fully human, and completely awake is to be continually thrown out of the nest. To live fully is to be always in no-man's-land, to experience each moment as completely new and fresh. To live is to be willing to die over and over again."

Pema Chödrön
When Things Fall Apart: Heart Advice for Difficult Times

"The first peace, which is the most important, is that which comes within the souls of people when they realize their relationship, their oneness, with the universe and all its powers, and when they realize that at the center of the universe dwells Wakan-Tanka, Great Spirit, and that this center is really everywhere, it is within each of us."

Black Elk
The Sacred Pipe: Black Elk's Account of the Seven Rites of the Oglala Sioux (1953), as told to Joseph Epes Brown

"Wisdom is knowing I am nothing, Love is knowing I am everything, and between the two my life moves."

Nisargadatta Maharaj

Dedication

I offer this flower to the lotus feet of Divine Mother and all sincere seekers as a blessing for our paths together in the Shared Heart.

I humbly thank my wife Sumire and my daughter Maia for all their support and love always.

Acknowledgments

This work has been possible only through the blessings of God and the masters.

I am eternally grateful for the spiritual guidance of Jesus and Mary, Yogananda and Babaji, the Dalai Lama and Avalokiteshvara Guan Yin in this lifetime.

My sincere appreciation to all who have helped this book get published.

To the editors, Shekinah El Daoud, Lightworker and Spiritual Mentor, and Trevor Taylor LLB (Hons), Award Winning Commonwealth Writer, the publishers Balboa Press, and Hay House.

My special thanks to Dr. Ranga Premaratna, Tareth and Suzie Farrow for spiritual support in the writing of this book.

God Bless You All

Love and Blessings
Guan Shi Yin

Preface

The most fundamental questions we have, focus on who we are, what are we doing here on this planet, what is our mission here and how we can achieve real lasting happiness.

'Diary of a Yogi' takes us on an inner journey of liberation and love, where we explore the twelve timeless portals of presence which have the power to transform our lives.

We are all on the path of self-realization, which is the greatest gift we have to offer this world.

We are all Buddhas, Christs, Krishnas and Divine Mothers and this immense power within us is the power of presence, a divine wisdom which can change our world, once we all act in unity consciousness.

Foreword

It is truly my delight and honour to write a few words about my "heart friend" in this lifetime and the incredibly beautiful and inspiring book of life and lifetimes produced with so much love and compassion.

We met many years ago in Mosman, Sydney and became close friends learning Reiki Jin Kei Do and the Buddho System of healing I teach.

In our journey as fellow travellers and students learning and teaching this unique gift of healing and transformation, we have shared many moments of amazing experiences.

I know that this book will transform the lives of many people and it's a privilege to be part of this journey and contribution to our world and universe, where a true bodhisattva appeared to be of light to us all".

Dr. Ranga Premaratna, Ph.D.

Fact

All the experiences, locations, organizations and people in this book are real.

Names of organizations and people have been changed to protect their privacy.

Introduction

The book you are about to read, 'Diary of a Yogi - A Book of Awakening,' is Altair Shyam's story, based on a series of true experiences, beginning with his mother Mary in the 1940s when she was just a young teenage girl, working in the orchards of Nelson in New Zealand. A Maori Elder approached her and began to tell her about her eldest son (Altair) and his past lives and future. Mary said she got such a fright she ran off never to return again.

When Altair was just two years old, he had a recurring dream that he was a Tibetan monk who died on a bridge just as described in the story within this book. He had the same dream every night for a year. Altair's parents were so worried as he woke up every night screaming. They took him to specialists until one doctor told them he was too hot, they took his blankets and clothes off and hey presto the dream stopped. But that was only the beginning of the many unbelievable experiences and meetings with remarkable people that Altair would have over his life.

Altair, described by his friends as a Forest Yoda, loves the stars and magic. As he journeys through struggles and hopes, miracles and danger across the world in search of answers to the mysteries of life he discovers more than anything else that our dreams do come true and they make us who we are when we have the courage to follow them.

Altair was inspired throughout his life by Christ, Krishna, Buddha, and the Divine Mothers, especially the Buddha of Perfect Compassion, Guan Yin. In One of Guan Yin's prior incarnations, as

Avalokiteshvara (Guan Yin in male form) She vowed that "Should She ever become disheartened in saving sentient beings, may Her body shatter into a thousand pieces." This is how great Her overwhelming Compassion truly was.

"One day, while helping beings in a higher realm, She looked down into the hells which She had emptied through the teaching of the Dharma, and realized, to Her dismay, that countless beings were still flooding into them. In a moment of exasperation, She became so disheartened that true to Her vow, Her body shattered in great agitation and despair. Despite this, She did not just give up — Her consciousness beseeched the Buddhas for help. Of the Buddhas who came to aid Her, one was Amitabha Buddha, who became Her Guru (personal teacher) Buddha within that Incarnation. With the Buddha's miraculous powers, She attained a new form — one with a thousand helping hands of Compassion coupled with a thousand eyes of Wisdom in each palm. With this, She renewed Her vow to saving not just limited sentient beings, but all sentient beings."

Those one thousand arms and those one thousand eyes each, in turn, became one thousand Bodhisattvas, you and me, human beings determined like Guan Yin to save all beings from suffering. When we begin our Bodhisattva or Earth Angel path of helping some beings, we are bound to be disheartened, due to our unperfected Compassion and Wisdom. We get impatient with others, frustrated and then angry with the world, we invite fear into our lives, and we turn away again and again from the Path in that disappointment. As we all suffer from spiritual burnout from time to time — let us then, be Bodhisattvas and Earth Angels to each other — and always help each other by reaching out from Our Shared Heart.

In Lak'ech Ala K'in - I am you, and you are me.

Love and soul blessings
Guan Shi Yin

About Guan Shi Yin

Guan Shi Yin is married with a daughter. She was named after Guan Yin, the Chinese Goddess of Compassion, by her father. After several years serving as a nun in large temples in East Asia including Shitenno-ji, Kiyomizu-dera and Shaolin temples, Guan Shi Yin was connected to Avalokiteshvara, the male embodiment of Guan Yin, through the Sakya Centers of Tibetan Buddhism in India. She left the temples in 2000 and has since been working in the health, healing and wellbeing industry. She met Altair Shyam very early on in his travels and their experiences and those of the remarkable people they met around the world form the main core of the book 'Diary of a Yogi - A Book of Awakening.' Guan Shi Yin is a pseudonym.

About Altair Shyam

Altair is a teacher, healer, and mystic guiding the way of love, unity and harmony for the New Gaia that we are co-creating. He teaches that we are the way and that our freedom to be our true self is the key to transformation.

"The miracles of God lie within us. We are the light. We are the temple of the one chakra. Our awakened infinite light body brings all our dreams into reality."

Altair comes to the transformational fields of healing and awakening with over 25 years of formal and intensive mindful and heartful training, a background in teaching and education, and degrees and certifications in counselling and alternative health, business and mindful and heartful education.

Altair began training in alchemy with St Germain and BOTA, a Western Mystery School, as a teenager, and is guided throughout his life by Yogananda, the Dalai Lama, Krishnamurti, Ramana Maharshi, Gurumayi and Sai Baba through a series of formal initiations and meetings.

Altair is the author of a best-selling book 'Health Wealth and Wisdom in the New Millennium' also known as 'Your New Future' as well as composer of the music series 'Innocence and Experience' and creator of an online international schools curriculum. He founded, owned and directed three educational institutions, and is co-creating the online portals of presence course, awakening into love, compassion, wisdom, and healing.

Altair was manager, and coordinating practitioner of a healing centre in Sydney, Australia, comprising doctors and Chinese doctors, physiotherapists, counsellors, healers, and psychics.

He has taught more than 2000 healers via 'The Practical Mystic,' a direct-service program, trained many educators, mental health professionals, and searching souls in simple healing practices and applications for life, and has been leading healing groups in Japan and internationally since the 1990s. He has been the sole trainer of a mindful schools' initiative in Japan over this past year.

In 1995, Altair was featured in "Songs to Heal the Heart," a program on Californian public television about a series of 'miracles' integrating alchemy, Tibetan medicine and Vedic counselling in the US and Canadian communities which he was coordinating at the time.

Altair is devoted to the Goddess of Compassion Guan Yin Avalokiteshvara and Divine Mother. Altair has trained to teacher level in many disciplines from Reiki Tibetan Jin Kei Do (the way of wisdom and compassion) to acupressure and Shiatsu, including being practitioner in reiki clinical trials in Australia and considers himself forever a humble student of the divine source.

Altair also works in performing arts in Japan in schools and communities (music, drama, dance and choral festivals) raising money for those children disadvantaged in education and living in disaster areas."

Profits from the book 'Diary of a Yogi' will be donated to the charity 'War Child' empowering children and young people in conflict areas by providing psychosocial support, stimulating education and protecting children from the ravages of war.

CHAPTER 1

Samye

Mary pressed her jade cross close to her heart and moved through the brightening morning, taking care to keep to the trees out of sight of the early-morning workers. It was surprisingly quiet. The three lines of apple trees, heavily laden with fruit, ran the length of the orchard and caught the rising sun glistening on their dew as if they were dressing themselves to be more attractive for the first pickers. Mary caught a glimpse of the Maori elder, a *tohunga,* walking toward her from afar in the light of the morning. She reached for an apple and looked back the other way, avoiding the glare, and stepped back along the path to the tallest tree. That part of the path was still in the gloom and decorated with golden lanterns inset with tiny silver candles whose flames flickered in the early-morning breeze. The seats along the path were oak, not pine, and reserved for special guests who loved to stop and sip the home-made apple cider.

Mary stopped beside the first bench and touched the wood gently. It gave off an amiable scent and a warmth like a friend beckoning her to sit with him or her.

"Everything will be okay," she whispered to herself.

She had encountered *tohungas* (elders) before and knew they were able to shift form and travel across worlds if they wished. It was just as her grandmother had said, just like the stories she had been told.

She only wants a minute, she reminded herself. *It can't be that bad. Stop worrying.*

But she held the jade cross more tightly against her chest. She strode ahead down the path and through the open door to the packing shed at the other end of the orchard.

No one here, she thought, ignoring the sign that said: "Wipe your feet." *Thank goodness for that.*

Settling herself on one of the old packing crates just inside the door to steady her nerves, Mary's eyes darted back and forth along the walls of the shed and out through the door. The only light came from the sun and settled quietly on an old, beat-up crucifix that hung on the wall above an equally old advertisement for the orchard's Gala apples, which the owner prided herself on. Mary had lived most of her life in the Far North, so this working holiday in the Deep South was a rare foray into the liberty of southern charm. She had never been away from home before and had never met an elder. She had thought that kind of meeting was reserved for more distinguished people than she was.

She stood up and looked around.

The light moved and settled on her shoulder.

"Can I go now?" She was talking out loud to St. Anthony. Whenever she was in trouble or worried, she would ask him for help.

She felt a warmth extend out from her heart as if the saint had placed his hands there.

"Okay, okay." She took a deep breath.

The room was big, with a pool table in one corner for smoko, or break time. The ashtray at one end was littered with cigarettes. Along one wall was a stack of crates for packing, stored about five high. A jar with drooping violets and chrysanthemums needed changing, its water browned with hints of green mold at the sides.

"They could do with a clean," she said under her breath.

She sat on an old leather armchair filled with newspapers that crackled as she sat. She pulled her legs up and hugged her knees to look at the last wall, the one adjacent to the door. There were family portraits going way back in the owner's history—at the far end, a fierce warrior wearing a long, feathered cloak with tattoos covering nearly all his body. He stared at her with *mana* and authority, powers she felt she didn't possess.

"What are you looking at?" she said in response. But before she could wonder if those eyes really saw anything at all, she heard a shuffle of feet wiping themselves on the mat outside the door.

She shrank down in the armchair and wished she could disappear. She couldn't hide, but she could be quiet. Very, very quiet.

The light seemed to change in the room as a woman entered. Mary was dazzled for a moment, so she could only focus on the woman's legs and bare feet. Slowly she made out an outline. She was very small, Mary thought.

Then a deep voice boomed, interrupting her thoughts, "*KIa ora*. Hello, Mary. My name is Alice."

It was the *tohunga*. Mary held her breath, not daring to move. She thought she could see another figure beside Alice but shook her head, thinking it must be her imagination.

"How do you know my name?" whispered Mary. The voice was small and didn't even sound like hers and shook a little.

"I expect you will understand all that in due course."

Mary just nodded.

"And you've brought the future for me?" smiled Alice, reaching out to take one of Mary's hands.

"Yes, well ... er, no, I didn't know exactly why we were meeting. You did say it wouldn't be for long."

"That's right, just a minute in your time ..."

"A minute in my time?" Mary could feel the old woman's grip tighten around her own.

Mary bent slightly, trying to wrest her wrist free from Alice's grasp, but she was curious about what the elder could see in her hands.

She watched as Alice began to trace the lines of her palm slowly and gracefully as if she were writing on water. Alice must have been in her seventies, but her nimble, light movements belied that fact. As she continued tracing, Mary's vision became hazy, and she became aware, as before, that there seemed to be a second figure in the room that separated from Alice and settled just next to her right shoulder.

Mary was tense with anxiety. She was scared of bats and birds and crowded elevators, so having such strange forces so close was both exciting and terribly unnerving.

"W—wh—who?" she stammered. But Alice seemed to have anticipated her question.

"Your son," said Alice.

Of all the things she could have said, this shocked Mary the most. She was just sixteen years old and at a private girls' boarding school, and she had been kept as far away from boys and men as her mother thought humanly possible. The idea of a son had never entered her mind until that moment.

"Would you like to see what will happen to him? He has a fortunate future if you can help him make it into one."

A great fear was welling up inside Mary. Alice was said to be involved in magical arts with charms and spells, and her father, Hupini, was reputed to be a wizard, a great medicine man with powers in *makutu* (the black arts). He had knowledge beyond normal humans and could kill an enemy at a distance simply by projecting his will. Mary was scared that if she got caught up in this, something awful might happen to her.

What she saw next, however, completely banished all fear from her mind.

Alice took some toetoe grass from her pocket and rubbed it on Mary's palm. Then she began to chant a prayer, a *karakia*, mumbling in low, soft tones that Mary could not understand.

As Alice spoke, continuing to rub deeper now, the grass turned into a white powder that filled the lines on Mary's palm. In front of Mary's eyes, the palm became a lattice of thin, white, flowing streams across a lush, pink land. Alice cupped Mary's hand in her own and poured the thin streams of powder into her own palm before releasing her grip on Mary. Alice then stirred the magical streams of powder in her hand with her other finger until they all dissolved into one miniature ocean in the valley of her palm. She threw this alchemical mixture up into midair and all over Mary.

Mary gave a shudder as the umbrella of water descended onto her, feeling for all the world as if a puddle had been dropped on her from heaven above. Alice mumbled one more word before turning and leaving through the door she had entered and gesturing for Mary to follow.

Mary was dumbfounded. Her thoughts were racing. What had she really seen? Was she bewitched? Where was Alice going?

"Wait!" she called, but it came out as a croak.

As she spoke, she heard shouting, a clamor steadily rising into a battle cry from the far end of the orchard. And the sound of bells. A terrible sound, not like the sound of a bell calling a congregation to church but of many bells clanging as people were bludgeoned to death.

"'Just a minute in my time,'" said Mary. "I thought we had more time than that."

For although she was swift getting to the door, Alice had vanished, and in her place was a scene of devastation.

The door, the one the elder had entered and left by, now opened onto a horizon torn ragged by dense, mottled, brown mountains.

The light grew more intense. The veils of time trembled and parted and unfolded above her and to left and right like curtains drawn back against the backdrop of the mountains. The arcs of light swirled around her, increasing in brilliance and magnificence right across the horizon and touching the lips of the sky itself. She could hear the hiss and fiery bellows of vast, unimaginable forces forging weapons for battle.

"Soldiers!" came a cry, not in her own tongue but in a language and voice that was both strange and yet familiar, and she knew with a mixture of joy and trepidation that it was the voice of her son.

Suddenly, a heavy hand knocked her forward, and she lost her breath and could only lean over and pant and gasp as bullets rang overhead, ricocheting off prayer bells. She was standing in the eggshell colored sands of a main courtyard in front of what seemed to be the main temple of a monastery. Its thick, whitewashed mud-brick walls were no defense.

"Impossible!" she thought in vain as another round of artillery fire clattered off the already heavily damaged doors of the temple's central gate.

Voices barked severe orders in strained voices. The monks around her were clearly trained for fighting as they moved into a defensive formation but they were hopelessly outnumbered and outgunned by the soldiers pouring through into the temple grounds from the streets beyond. Soldiers that were heavily armed against the monks, many who only wielded farming implements and short kitchen knives. The monks could only fight at close range, and so they waited, vulnerable to snipers and attacks from the air. Though the monks exploded with fury when the soldiers came closer, so many fell, wasted lives and helpless victims in a rebellion that was not of their choosing.

Mary was dragged back inside the temple gates and crouched low inside against the thick wooden doors with their beautiful brass ornaments. An arcade swept along the interior wall alive with ancient pictures of many Buddhas. Painted in extraordinary detail with flower petals that gently melded together and Buddha's robes folding so precisely and intricately, Mary watched in horror as the first wave of Chinese soldiers defaced the frescoes as they ran past, gouging and hacking the faces of every Buddha from the plaster.

Mary looked up at the sky and gasped as fire burst from the air and artillery shells smashed into the columned prayer and chanting hall. The hall faced a huge altar of Buddhist symbols flanked by eight towering gold painted images of the Buddha. Tiny yellow flames in front of each statue flickered and then died out as if signaling the death knell of the heart of the temple, as the innumerable brass bowls brimming with cloudy yak butter were pitched and tossed into the carnage. The thick sweet scent was mixed with blood and the toxic fumes of the spent artillery shells hanging heavy in the dim light.

If she thought she had time to get her bearings she was mistaken, as another shell burst through the wall on the opposite side of the courtyard and opened to a vista of squat stark low stone buildings. Sporadic leafless trees skewering the landscape burst into flames as the soldiers passed.

In the direction the shell had come from Mary saw many platoons of soldiers coming to join the ones already looting the temple, and in the radiance of the light she was tugged headlong out of the fray and over a bridge where she saw her son. She heard a sound that struck her heart with dread. A terrifying scream. Her son. The soldiers, standing in formation to block any exit from the bridge, had opened fire.

As Mary watched, a bright line marked the track of the bullet that pierced her son's heart. He pitched off the side of the bridge and fell into the river below and was borne away. The soldiers were following so quickly that they swept past her as if she was a ghost. Their real target was the temple at the center of the monastery. They ran straight on without hesitating or turning to the side.

More artillery shells flew overhead ripping straight through the remaining walls and devastating the enclosure within.

None of this mattered to Mary. The Light was becoming transparent and the veil between her own time and that horrid memory was thinning. Her heart felt like stone, and her body was heavy. Little figures were running through the monastery, as bodies tottered and ran and were cut down in flames. The temple was a mass of twisted wood and metal, a pall of smoke rising from its centre.

The bridge clearly felt the weight of the carnage and creaked, cracked and then collapsed into the river after her son.

Mary was no longer on the bridge, but she wasn't in the river either.

"Goodbye my son," she said although she didn't know where the words came from, it could have been an older Mary that was speaking. "I have to go back across now, but I will find you, again."

Her heart thumping painfully with love, Mary turned away and flew up, and reaching out felt a hand, the Elder, encouraging her onward.

"That is where your son will die, 17 years from now in 1959, on the bridge across the River Tsangpo to the Samye Monastery in Tibet."

There was a loud crash as the last remnants of that horrid scene below fell into an abyss.

Mary was floating, perfectly still. She looked down and found her body, lying prone, in the sunlight of the orchard morning. The veil was still there, and she didn't want to return, but she made a big effort, pushing until she was gliding just above her body, one step, then another and then she leaped to the far side with all her strength. She landed with a soft thump and then a whoosh like all the air being taken out of her. Her body heaved, and she took a big breath.

After a moment she opened her eyes and dug her nails into the fresh earth to make sure she was home. There was no way back. The *tohunga* stood some way off, then nodded to acknowledge her, turned and vanished into the trees.

Mary was alone.

CHAPTER 2

Zahor

Altair woke and seeing his mother Mary's laughing face, began to laugh too. Mary pretended to hide, and every time she reappeared it made Altair laugh harder, until he laughed so hard that he got hiccups.

She made soft shooshing noises patting him gently on the back, until he burped up the air and lay back in her arms with an angelic demeanor.

Mary and Altair were besotted with each other. Everything about the other was perfect and delightful.

"Time to sleep, little darling. I shouldn't have woken you sweetheart."

Altair was the son of a hospital manager and a hospital matron. At just two years old he began to lucidly dream which frightened him out of his wits. He had the same dream, night after night for an entire year, a dream in which he was a monk on a bridge, falling off into a chasm. The dream always ended the same way, with an enchanted sound, like Om. Altair was a very curious, gentle child with a slight build not unlike a Yogi and curly brown hair which made him look like Apollo, a nickname his elementary school teachers called him. The school lay directly opposite his house. He had many good friends but he was happiest gazing into the stars, and so he wrote to NASA when he was five years old asking to be an astronaut on the first one-way trip to Alpha Centauri which he had noticed was the closest star to where he was now. NASA responded by inviting Altair to join them when he was eighteen which only encouraged him to go deeper into researching the planets and the stars for signs of life, a habit which would pay dividends many years later when he bumped into a real extraterrestrial being.

Like every star child, Altair managed to find exactly who he needed to at exactly the right time in his life, while he went about the daily tasks of eating and sleeping, going to school and doing his homework. When he was thirteen the blessing in his life was Hannah, and he recognized her by a blue light that shone around her. The blue light appeared in front of him every time a truth or important signpost, which I call a light post, or significant person would appear. A light post is a sign on your path that you really should not miss, a sign that you have deliberately planted upon agreement with that person or truth, prior to incarnating here, so that you would know them when you met them. It may not be a blue light like Altair's. Sometimes it is an uncanny feeling that you have both met each other before. Hannah was in her twenties, tall, goddess-like, with golden-red hair that shone like spun gold. She wore her hair long and smiled with a radiance that would have shattered the heaviest darkness. She was graceful and assured and loved to hear Altair play the flute. "Do you like Mozart?" she would ask, which of course was Altair's favorite composer and "Won't you stay for tea?" she would insist, once they had finished playing a duet, with Hannah on her baroque recorder.

From the first time he met Hannah, Altair was convinced she was an alchemist or magician. He tried to ignore it, but some of the goings-on at the house next door, which was where Hannah lived, were far too mysterious to put aside for long. One day Altair was stricken by a strange illness. It felt like a fever that did not belong to him, as if he were bearing the burden of some forgotten time or place.

"What's wrong?" said Hannah when she saw him, crossing the road from the school playground, pale as a church mouse. "Something has got hold of me," said Altair despairingly, "and I can't shake it!" He looked downcast. Hannah just smiled one of her radiant smiles. "Never you mind. Go and have a short nap. Close the door and make sure you are not disturbed. Think of me. I will be with you." Altair went and did as she had told him. From the moment his head hit the pillow a most curious sensation overwhelmed him. Colors of the rainbow began moving up his body, caressing his skin, beginning with the soles of his feet. As the rainbow body surrounded him, he was transported to a garden, where he lay in repose, barely breathing, as the circles of light softly nurtured and healed him. He could hear Hannah's voice, or someone that sounded like her, gently soothing and easing away all the aches and pains. "Zahor" the voice intoned. He drifted away as if he were a feather on a breeze, riding on God's breath. The next sound he heard was his mother's voice. "Altair, Altair, are you alright?" He opened his eyes feeling his body as he scanned it top to toe. Not one ache, pain or feverish complaint remained.

Altair and his brothers and sisters lived a short walk from the beachfront, some distance from the great city, and contented themselves with boats and boat races. The city stood with a great tower, which was like a castle in the sky and so was called Sky City. Altair lived opposite the Convent, or so it was known, as it housed the Sisters of St Joseph, who went daily about their holy business, which included giving Altair piano lessons and striking his knuckles with a holy ruler when he struck the keys with lazy fingers. Altair's house, known as the railway station, because all manner of creatures from humans to dogs and ducks converged there, bordered by a stream with trout and that backed on to an orchard with horses, which they could ride if they asked politely, and pinch apples and oranges from the neighbors' trees if they didn't ask at all. Altair and his brother built forts down the back, hidden in the trees, and waged wars with the neighboring boys, which on one unfortunate occasion ended with his brother being blinded, temporarily mind you, on account of a vicious grapefruit thrown smack in his eye. Altair's heart missed a beat that day. He loved his brother Simon dearly. Altair and his brother were reckless. They climbed icy mountains in gumboots and shorts, made counterfeit money to fool the local greengrocer, and crafted makeshift rafts to steal aboard luxury yachts in the harbor to have private parties with their friends. In a manner of speaking, they felt for all the world like pirates and adventurers, willing to take what treasure and captives came their way, and sail into the wide blue yonder.

Altair enjoyed his life by the sea. For the most part, to an external observer, he appeared to be a boy attending middle school, but to the inward witness he was a detective following a trail. A path to the stars and beyond.

Altair became so interested in the stars that Hannah introduced him to a world-famous astrologer called Phillip. Altair's ears pricked up when she first offered to take him for a visit. Hannah had so many unusual friends. The sisters Raphael and Gabrielle on the other side of her house who had statues of Sai Baba that bled oil and gold dust they called vibhuti or sacred ash. The old friend Greg who looked rather like a warlock with pointy ears, highly arched eyebrows and an even more pointed beard, whose entire life had been foretold in a book of leaves called 'The Book of Bhrigu.' 'The Book of Bhrigu,' or Bhrigu Samhita, is an ancient manuscript made of palm leaves, and the family in Punjab that owns it, has been visited by countless politicians and film stars over the last sixty years. The manuscript tells the fortunes of the soul, past, present and future manifestations, and those like Greg who visited, are stunned to find not only their names, but their parents and grandparents and a detailed sketch of their present life as well. Whenever Hannah asked Altair to accompany her, he would put down whatever he was doing, sit at her side and listen intently to the tales of magic from around the world. So, when he sat in front of Phillip he was most surprised to hear this famed oracle pronounce "You have the makings of a famous astrologer" and then go on to tell Altair all he already knew about the fragile world of a thirteen-year-old and a lot more besides. Altair never had the aim of being rich. He was content with finding happiness and passing on what he could to other people. He knew he was lucky because a luck dragon had breathed on him early on in life and charms and treasures literally would fall in his lap. A luck dragon is like a lucky charm. It is particularly fond of children and if you are lucky enough to find one it will grant you never-ending wishes, like magic. Altair wished for happiness and his childhood was just like that, filled with golden moments, protected by his luck dragon. If he had known of the Chintamani Stone, the wish-fulfilling jewel in both the Hindu and Buddhist traditions, said to be the equivalent of the Philosopher's Stone, he might have been persuaded to use "wish-fulfilling jewel" as a nickname for his luck dragon. He would know more about the Chintamani Stone, when he was lucky enough to be given one, many years later, out of the heart of a statue of the Goddess of Compassion Guan Yin. For now, that was something most thirteen-year-old boys didn't bother themselves about.

Altair's path, as he would later find out, lay between the stars and magic. Hannah would introduce him to both of these, most unexpectedly, and all at once.

The path of magic, he was to find, lay just over the fence and down the winding path, past the *pohutukawa* tree resplendent with crimson blossoms like toothbrush bristles, and up a single flight of steps to Hannah's library set among musical instruments and paintings of tarot keys and the tree of life. The alchemist herself was working on the blueprint for the philosopher's stone on this particular day, the pattern on the trestleboard and the book 'The Kybalion' which is how Altair would first learn the seven principles of alchemy. In between these tasks she was bringing up her daughter and attending to daily matters of the household, which included keeping an eye on the family debt, incurred through the wayward hands of her gambling husband. To make ends meet, the alchemist was sewing elegant garments for wealthy clients, and the chitter chatter of the spool of thread on the winding bobbin was the noise that greeted Altair as he entered.

"I want to learn magic!" Altair burst out, unable to contain himself any longer.

Hannah got up slowly from her seat and walked over to the library.

"I've been waiting a long time for you to ask," she said, pulling two books from the library and handing them to Altair.

The first book had the most gracious face Altair had ever seen staring out from the cover.

"Who is this?" he said pointing to the godly person in orange robes.

"Yogananda," said Hannah as if Altair should know.

"A Yogi."

That simple word sent shivers up and down Altair's spine.

"The other book is 'The Kybalion'. It opens the door to all the forces that govern the universe. Mastery of those forces enables you to do alchemy and become an alchemist."

Altair looked at the small book in black, with gold inscription on the cover and a symbol of a triangle with three concentric circles as its seal.

"Borrow them, for as long as you like," said Hannah.

"Then come and ask him some questions," she said, pointing to the door.

"Him?" Did Hannah mean Michael, her gambling husband? Altair felt a growing excitement as he turned to go, walking towards the door of the library, clutching the two books in his hand.

Perhaps she'd been joking, and she'd meant Phillip the astrologer. He was far more interesting and more likely to be able to answer some of the questions Altair wanted to ask. Perhaps he was through the door.

Altair stopped and stared. By the time he reached the door of the library he felt the hairs on the nape of his neck stand on end as he found himself walking into a crowd of people he didn't recognize. He was blindfolded with semi-transparent silk and holding a staff and the crowd on either side of him were staring at him, willing him to go on.

Now Altair was nervous. He looked for Hannah and to his relief he noticed her, dressed in a white tunic, he knew it was her by her long golden-red hair. But when she looked at him her eyes were a deep green, like emerald, rather than her usual hazel color.

The pyramid he was walking into, for that is what it was, was lit by Dendera lamps, which illuminated the inner temple and the faces of what looked like priests and priestesses, although the main focal point, perhaps an altar, was hidden in darkness. The people lined the route to that point, and in front there was a beautiful carved throne. Altair paused at the edge of the crowd as a large man appeared from the shadows and came forward to meet him. A ripple of anticipation ran through the crowd as he threw a powdery substance into the air. Altair felt light-headed as a series of visions unfolded in front of him. An ocean, a garden, a palace, three lovers. The man was tall and bald and round-faced with an air of mystique. He wore a simple white tunic with a gold band around his waist and he was bare-chested from the waist up with two serpentine rings encircling each arm. Altair recognized the aura the man gave off. It was someone used to wielding power, a lord, a pharaoh or a king.

"That's Master R, whom some call St. Germain," whispered the voice of the woman who looked like Hannah, now beside him. "You can take your blindfold off now."

Master R began to speak in a low rumbling voice.

"Welcome initiates of the Holy Temple. We've come here to listen and see. All of you who walk the path of pathlessness have lost something or someone dear to you to get here. Even if that is your Self. We are under no illusions. The path from the dark places to the light requires great courage, perseverance and resilience.

We have in front of us a new initiate who like all of us is also an Old One. His name is Altair Shyam and he is being sought by the

Dark. By the forces of ignorance and separation. He is in our care now and it is up to us to guide him with love and wisdom."

Altair felt his face go hot and his palms begin to tingle. He wanted to hide. He turned to Hannah for reassurance.

"To bring about great change we need to take big actions," continued Master R. "The dark is rising, and the forces of ignorance are sweeping this world which in its turn opens portals to the ignorance of other worlds. We don't know which way the tide will turn. All we do know is that if we don't take immediate action the opus on love will cease its writing.

For every action there is an equal and opposite reaction. We know that in as much as we have great Masters throughout our earth's history, Source Messengers who have guided us, we also have equally powerful agents of the dark, who infiltrate our religions and governments and security forces to breed fear, divisive views and hatred. We know it's going on, we see it and we are now in a better place than in all our human history to do something about it on a global level.

For every decision there is a price, a sacrifice. I am suggesting that we take a united stand and fill the corridors of power with young people like Altair, angels of the light, who are willing to stand and speak up and fight for peace and love and light."

There was a murmur, then a roar of approval from the crowd, the roar turning into a clamor which shook the foundations of Altair's world. The walls of the pyramid shook, and the capstone of the pyramid appeared to fall inwards, collapsing the whole structure in upon itself. Altair felt the same lightheadedness grasping at him, until all at once he found himself back in the library, facing the figure now standing in front of him, silhouetted in the hallway.

"Go ahead," said Hannah. "Ask anything you want. He's waiting for you. You don't have long before he has to go."

Altair hesitated. The Master R was stern and yet kind, a pillar of light and also a bastion of hope. Altair held out his hand.

"Welcome to the family of light," said Master R.

Altair felt like the sky was about to crumble and fall. The Master's voice was like a sound he remembered as a young toddler of two years old, the Om, rumbling like the voice of God in a chasm.

"Thank you," was all Altair could manage.

"So, has Hannah here been teaching you properly?"

"Oh yes, we play flute and recorder often."

"Ah, including an insight into the rainbow body I believe?"

The library was a beautiful spacious room with a fireplace, laced curtains which allowed just the right amount of light in and an oval oak table with six chairs.

Without quite knowing how, Altair found himself guided into one of the chairs with the Master R sitting at the head of the table and Hannah sitting opposite. Hannah was a beautiful distraction to the stern Master whose eyes seemed to bore into Altair's very soul.

Altair found a drink in front of him that he was sure wasn't there previously. It was a nectar, warm and soothing, which he gratefully drank to settle his nerves.

"So, you fell off the bridge into a chasm," said the Master, with no segue.

"Yes."

"And you were running away from …"

"I wasn't running … I was charging, into a battle … for …"

"The Dalai Lama. At Samye. Samye Monastery."

"Yes, I've known him before, many times, in different … forms … and I was in this garden …"

"Zahor, the western gardens of Princess Mandarava's palace in the kingdom of Zahor."

"My name was …"

"Palmo Shonu. You were sixteen when you met her."

"I knew astrology."

"You were an adept."

"A Saraswati initiate."

"Skilled in Jyotish astrology."

"I was her astrologer, Princess Mandarava!"

"In the time of Padmasambhava and Yeshe Tsogyal, yes. You read symbols as you do now. Each person has a light body, a rainbow body that is a portal to all wisdom and understanding. It can be triggered or activated in so many ways. One of them is by understanding and reading the symbols in the matrix of their chart."

Altair was swept back in time to the gardens of Zahor in an instant. It was like watching a movie running in full sensory vision in his head.

"I remember. I was in the western gardens with many people from all parts of Zahor and beyond. There was a monk called Arnapa. People were asking him all sorts of questions, but his answers only led to more confusion. So, I asked him where he had trained to develop his knowledge. He took this as an insult and said a young sixteen-year-old girl like myself was no better than a rambling magpie. I explained that the esoteric instructions on astrology are like a wish-fulfilling jewel. That the wisdom text of Saraswati is as melodious as the sound of the vina. The composition is as beautiful as a dance of art on paper. To make contact with the light through the stars is to perfect transcendent primordial wisdom. It is the precious doctrine of the Buddha."

"He tried to belittle you," said Hannah.

"He was the reason Princess Mandarava noticed me. She told her mother the Queen that she wished me to be her teacher in the art of astrology. Her parents did not want a commoner to instruct her so asked a holy man to consult with them. He recognized me as a Dakini, a sky dancer or tantric priestess and said it would be good for me to stay permanently with the princess. I was invited to the palace, became a member of her entourage and taught her everything I knew about astrology. We studied art and music and dance and magic together. I remained close to her thereafter."

"He made you stand up for the light. Suffering has the potential to uncover the deepest light. Just as you are doing now with the Brotherhood, the agents of the dark. Standing up for the rights of children wherever you are. Even though you are persecuted."

"Persecuted?" Altair had to think for a moment about what the Master R meant.

"Yes, that same instinct that made you fight against the accusations of Arnapa is the same energy protecting you today against the Brotherhood that has infiltrated religious organizations and schools, security agencies and Hollywood celebrity circles, political groups and financial regulators as you will find out. Your rebellion comes from seeking the truth."

"Well, kids know how to sniff out the Brotherhood and thankfully I know which ones to stay away from. They pretend to be guiding kids when they are in fact manipulating them."

Master R nodded.

"One day I went on a walk with one of the teachers and he touched me and I said, "Get away from me," and hit his hand off my shoulder which ended up in a rose bush with thorns and he said, "I will make sure you fail all my classes," so I quit. I was so angry but didn't know how to express it. My father and mother could not understand as that was my favorite class, physics, and I was the top student. Sadly, that teacher committed suicide after his relationship with another young boy was revealed.

And now I see it happening to children and women all over the world, what I experienced. The rape of children and women, physically and emotionally. I want to help."

"These people will meet with terrible karma and be answerable to their maker," said the Master.

Altair sat back against the chair and looked at Hannah. She was smiling at him, a rich, graceful smile filled with affection and kind expectation. The Master R still had that stern look of deepest wisdom that left Altair feeling exposed.

"Tell us how you wish to help and what it is that you see," said Master R.

At that the floodwaters broke. Almost on the Master's command Altair's vulnerability and his own deep wisdom was revealed as if all the veils were pulled back at once to reveal a bright day with wondrous shadows and textures of light and insight.

Altair saw wonders he could only gape and marvel at. He knew what he was seeing. The Djedhi Way, the path of the priesthood of Ancient Egypt. The priests specialized in intensive meditation techniques of mastering the flow of the Holy Spirit energies through points along the spinal column, using the same techniques as Krishna and Babaji, Buddha, Jesus, the Essenes, the Order of the Temple of Solomon and the modern Templar Order. Those energies were awake right now, opening a portal to the past, present and future. Altair could see so many aspects of the wisdom on his path.

A Light Dolphin Isle in the Pleiades. Harvesting sea plankton in the light ponds of Atlantis. A Naga Serpent of Wisdom. A meeting with Krishna. Playing with Moses when he was but a babe and being an acolyte under Lady Nada in the Judaean Desert rituals. Meeting Buddha and Manjushri on the road to Sarnath. Standing at the foot of the cross looking up at Jesus with Mary Magdalene. Casting out demons. Alchemy in the Source Group of Merlin with Tareth. Meeting Padmasambhava and Yeshe Tsogyal in India and in Tibet with Princess Mandarava. Doing Bodhisattva social work for Masters Kukai and Gyoki in Japan. Studying Tao and Zen under Master Huang Po. Sailing as a wayfarer from Maui. An adviser to Sakya Pandita. A Raj in Northern India. Serving the Fifth Dalai Lama as Sakya Pema, again an astrological adviser. And then with the Master R as St. Germain before the fall off the bridge into the chasm in 1959. Then further, beyond the now, Altair saw into a time on Mt. Potalaka with Guan Yin, the astral worlds of Hiranyaloka with Yogananda and Ketumati with Maitreya.

"It's a continuum Altair," said Hannah in her musical voice. "We've all met before."

"The Shared Heart," said Master R.

"Love," said Altair.

"The Golden Thread woven through all universes," said Hannah.

"The attractive principle," said Master R. "The quintessential law of attraction."

"So why target women and children, and vulnerable young boys?"

"The power of attraction, innocence and love, is strongest when we are young. Young and free, not bound or possessed. Sacred and pure. It takes a great deal of courage and practice to maintain that power of attraction as we get older. There are so many distractions."

"So, if we maintain that innocence and purity, that awareness of love, we can see across worlds and into and beyond time like I did just now?"

"Yes, that is why the dark wants to tamper with the consciousness of the young. It stops them from seeing the truth, from understanding their real power. It stops them from knowing that they are already free."

"Now Altair," said Hannah, "I'm going to tell you something. The Master R has been following the progress of many young people for a long time. People with a message. Young people like yourself."

Altair swallowed. He felt like someone was about to hand him an ancient text to read, a book filled with magic and infinite possibilities, stories of the stars, the realms of gods and goddesses, a book of love. And with it came immense responsibility.

"He knew about you as a child. From a baby. We knew about your visions, your dreams. We arranged for your mother to place you in the tender care of a mother superior."

"Mother Therese?" She had been Altair's favorite source of all things wise for as long as he could remember. It was she who had told him he was placed under the protection of the Virgin Mary, and she who had taught him the powers of Jesus and the archangels.

"We don't know what your parents have told you, but they don't know the whole truth of it."

"You know you can cast out demons."

Altair was dazed.

"You can heal."

"See the future."

"Speak to dolphins, snakes, and beings from other worlds."

"You can project your Self across worlds. That is how you will call beings from other worlds to visit this planet. You can harness the kundalini force, shakti, completely naturally. To call the ocean to rise and help you, you have to become the ocean. The simple practice of the sacred breath and Kriya Yoga as you will find in Yogananda's book has all you need to accomplish it."

"You will help thousands of people simply by sharing the power of faith. By believing in them and showing them that a 3000-year-old ancient manuscript speaks from across time and space about their life path and purpose. You will awaken in them the power to be free, to go and live their true purpose."

"This is the truth about you Altair, and so many others like you. You were not put here by accident. You chose, along with many others, to meet here, and change the world. Not just this world. But many others. You have many gifts to help others. What have you discovered?"

"Well, there is this," said Altair and he reached out to touch the hands of both Master R and Hannah.

"The blue light," and the blue light he had been able to see from his childhood, to his amazement, coursed up both his arms and into the room around them filling the old library.

"The Blue Pearl," said the Master R, "as it is often known, is a sign of things to come. A message from other worlds. A light from Guan Yin. Swami Muktananda described how it expanded in front of him, engulfed him and carried him to other worlds. It is a physical manifestation of the soul and contains all consciousness in it."

"Do you know how to use it to its fullest potential yet?" asked Hannah.

"I have been able to see it since I was very little. It is a sign of truth. It appears whenever anyone speaks the truth or when I meet people that are an important part of my path. It appears in my head and with my eyes open. Sometimes it is a bright iridescent flash, like magnesium."

"It's a truth-measure and a form of the inner Self. It contains all the different dimensions of existence," said Master R. "It is a sign of Christ consciousness."

"Everyone can see it with practice," said Hannah. "You just have a naturally developed extrasensory perception."

"A rare faculty," said Master R, "to see it in one so young. Muktananda was also an adept and initiate of the Saraswati Order just like you. You have meditated a lot in this life and previous ones. With such consistency and love of meditation, shakti, the power of the Source of All in the universe awakes inside you. It created the outer universe and when you are still you can connect with it and it awakens within you an inner universe of bliss and happiness. As without so within. Try it now. Close your eyes. Focus on your breath. Breathing in, breathing out. Be still and know God. Trust your feelings, trust the Source. The energy and consciousness that flows within you flows in all things you perceive around you and outside you. As within so without. When we get our self out of the way, when we surrender to what is, the Source alone is."

"I see light, everywhere. I feel the universe flowing, everywhere. I see the Blue Pearl, everywhere."

"Muktananda, like many great masters, planted the seed of awakening in you long ago, just as Yogananda did. That knowledge has kept you safe until you were old enough to use its power to help others. The agents of the dark are tests for you and others like you, to help restore the balance. Where there is strong light there is equally strong darkness.

Now the churches and religions and science are moving towards unity but there is an equally strong conservative movement that wants to keep things separate and will do anything it can to stop it.

The experiences that occur in our life path are designed to make us stronger and our choices are simply to bring us to the point of ultimate freedom. Where we can let go and embrace all that is. Life and death, love and fear, peace and suffering.

The blue light and the Blue Pearl are given to us to act as beacons to awaken the light in others.

They are gifts, never to keep, but to uncover wisdom and lead each of us to our purpose, our true destiny.

So, keep it secret and keep it safe.

There will come a time when you will need it to assist you on your next journey as you leave this body and it departs with you. That is the true meaning of deathlessness or immortality."

Altair noticed the Master R had cupped his hands and from within his palms a beautiful Blue Pearl radiated with unearthly light. He folded his hands over and reached across the table and placed his hands on Altair's. Altair felt suddenly very shy of this immensely powerful man, with his stern look and eyes which pierced to his soul.

"It is time for me to return. You have a lot to think about and absorb. Take care Altair."

"Thank you," said Altair, clutching the Blue Pearl to his heart with one hand and taking the two books with his other.

Master R and Hannah smiled.

Altair's mother was waiting at the side door of the house in Lake Road when he entered.

"You were gone a long time," she said. "I was about to call you for tea."

"Sorry Mum," said Altair. And he gave her a big hug and kissed her on the cheek before settling down to tuck into the big Lancashire hotpot Mary had prepared for them all.

CHAPTER 3

Eden

Altair had no easy time adjusting to this new information. To be told one can heal is one thing but to know that he was able to call beings from another star to visit is quite another. Altair knew his path lay between stars and magic. He just didn't know quite how that would come about yet.

Altair didn't get time to worry about that for long as there were school days to fill with music and art and books. His favorites, now placed with honor alongside 'Autobiography of a Yogi' and 'The Kybalion', were 'Lord of the Rings', Joyce's 'Portrait of the Artist as a Young Man' and Michener's 'The Drifters'.

Before three years were up he had mastered a number of instruments and was about to start his first band. That band had a lot of fans, especially young girls, one of whom was DJ. She was in a gang of some notoriety and that was when all the trouble started.

"One evening we were messing with an Ouija board just for fun," she told Altair amidst hysterical tears, "and the glass started moving of its own accord. It was possessed!" She continued sobbing. "The glass spelt out one of our names. It totally freaked us out, so we smashed the glass. Woke up the neighbors who thought we were having a fight. That's when it happened. To Carl. He's in the Mad

Ave gang too. So, on his way home he hit a telephone pole. Not another car on the whole street. He's in hospital."

"What sort of car?"

"His dad's! So, his family found out and now they're real mad at all of us. They think we caused it. They don't know how awful we feel!

So, the rest of us were in a fix then, coz we thought this thing must be coming for us. And sure enough, Alan, that's Carl's friend, he tried to steal the church's offertory one Sunday after mass and the cops came and he got arrested."

"So, what did you do?"

"It got worse," DJ took a heavy breath and her head slumped. "John is in critical care."

"Were you with him?" John was DJ's boyfriend.

"Yes," was all DJ could say and the tears kept flowing down her cheeks and wouldn't stop.

"I'm next," DJ said finally. "John took an overdose and I'm next."

DJ was Samoan and came from a large family of Catholics. Psychic experiences were the norm rather than the exception. But black magic was black magic. Altair knew DJ's family would have frowned on her excursions into Ouija boards. She would not get any support from them. Suddenly a strong conviction came over him. He felt Master R's words weaving through and dispelling DJ's fear. Healing, casting out demons, freeing people by giving them faith.

"You'll be OK," said Altair. "And if you get frightened again come back and I'll see if I can help you." He told DJ what the Master had promised he would be able to do.

"Healing? I want to learn that too. There's so much I want to do. I don't want to die! I'm too young! We only did the Ouija board as a joke. We never meant to cause anyone any harm! You're such a good person. Why did I ever get mixed up in this?" DJ managed to calm down after lots of breathing.

"You'll be OK."

She nodded and left.

Altair was convinced DJ would be fine, but he had the feeling this wasn't the end of it.

That night when he was alone he said his prayers and sat down to do his daily meditation. Since reading Yogananda's book he had started the lessons with Yogananda's Foundation and he was also practicing alchemy through the lessons of Master R's Builders. This gave a strong foundation for the feeling he had that his path to the stars and magic was unfolding surely and clearly. He had also begun a study of both Eastern and Western astrology so on this night he was contemplating how to unify these philosophies and practices.

Remembering what Yogananda had said about divine consciousness and being receptive to what the divine sends you, or doesn't, Altair focused his mind on meditation, prayer and alchemy and the symbols of the stars. He found that if he truly relaxed with awareness by practicing the AUM technique and breathing calmly, new visions and insights would come.

Tonight, the only message he received was to go to sleep. DJ was on his mind. Her fear and worry whirled round in his mind like a playground roundabout. He found if he didn't avoid it but embraced it like a warm cuddly cat then its energy would shift, and he could appreciate its angles and glimpse its deeper meaning for both DJ and himself. So, he decided to go to sleep.

He was no sooner asleep then a shaft of light brighter than the sun struck his room and he awoke to a radiant presence. The majestic light poured from an eternal source blazing and blinding him. It sent a thrill through his body of something far beyond anything he had known, heralding the arrival of someone who was always there for him, a powerful presence and joy he had always felt since a baby when Mother Therese and his own mother Mary had first whispered the words "baby Jesus" to him. That same deep thrill filled his heart with joy as Jesus appeared in the room, radiating the dazzling light of the Christ Consciousness from his Sacred Heart and said to him

"Be healed according to your faith."

And

"By the power of Christ begone."

In that moment and forever more Altair knew that he would never fear death or demons or the world of the dark because the light that shone on the darkness was so much greater.

Altair sank back into his bed with a sigh and fell immediately into a deep sleep.

Several days later, with much coming and going, friends visiting and relatives dropping by, there came an evening when his parents were out helping a family of Cambodian refugees, charity work they had all done for years. His mother Mary received the Queen's medal for her service to several hundred Cambodian families in placing them in jobs and houses in the community so a sudden trip to help someone in need was not out of the ordinary. The house was empty which seemed scarcely possible. Altair was sitting on the sofa when there was a knock at the door.

"DJ!"

DJ could barely get up the grey steps and through the double doors. She looked like she was weighed down with a burden. As she came through the door Altair noticed a slight shift in the air, as if something ominous was attaching itself to DJ.

"It's got hold of me," said DJ as she sunk down into the sofa.

"What is it?" said Altair even though he felt he knew.

"A demon," said DJ and slumped even lower, her hair falling forwards and her face sinking into her hands. She began to cry. Big whale tears the size of olives welled up and stalked down her cheeks. "Do you know why it is harming us?"

Altair didn't know but he could guess. The agents of the dark were cunning and manipulative. They bred on fear and vulnerability and loved to meddle. They preyed on young people who exposed themselves to the unknown through drugs or black magic without knowing what they were dealing with. They were insidious and deadly dangerous.

"Lie down," said Altair. "I can help you. Close your eyes."

DJ sighed and lay down. Her face was damp with sweat and her eyes were glazing over. Altair looked at DJ. She was lying very still. He placed his hands on her forehead to begin. He had no real idea of what to do. Just follow his heart and trust in Jesus.

DJ's breath was very shallow. It began to follow an uneven pattern with ragged gasps. Altair moved one of his hands from her forehead to her heart.

Then he said in a very loud voice.

"By the power of Christ, begone!"

DJ shuddered. Her body tightened as if she were going to have a fit, her breath came in gasps and her eyes closed tighter in pain.

Altair cried aloud again,

"By the power of Christ, begone!"

DJ's body began to spasm. She frothed at the mouth. The room filled with dark wild shapes and sounds that created confusion and fear.

Altair stayed steadfast and said a third time in a commanding voice,

"By the power of Christ, begone!"

DJ gave a fearful cry, groaned and was still.

Above Altair's head there was a burst of light and for an instant he could see the radiant face of Jesus. Tears of gratitude filled his eyes and he remained for long moments with his hands on DJ's forehead and heart before removing them.

DJ had sunk into a deep sleep. She didn't wake for nearly an hour and a half and when she did she looked at Altair with soft, comprehending eyes.

"Thank you," was all she could say. "It's gone."

Then she left. She was never bothered by demons or evil spirits again.

That night Altair lay in the comfort of his bed in the east wing of the house. It was a bitter night with heavy clouds, swirling winds and driving rain.

Suddenly something hurtled out of the dark and struck his window. It sent his heart into a flutter of shock. He got up to peer out of his window into the darkness. It was like a sharp pain, buzzing and murderous, trying to fill his head with confusion and fear. As his sleepy eyes adjusted he saw it. A face, black, angry and furiously trying to get in the window. It scratched and clawed on the smooth glass. It was so monstrously angry Altair thought it would break the glass. It had two gaping holes for eyes and a twisted malevolent mouth. It saw Altair and Altair saw it. And in that moment, he spoke.

"By the power of Christ, begone!"

And with a flash of light burning bright in the darkness like magnesium set to a flame the creature vanished with a howl.

Of all the colleges in the Sky City, Altair's was the largest. It was built around a mountain and was coveted for its sports fields and its musical heritage. The chapel was at its center, and not far from there Brother Stephen could be found narrating stories of heroes in Latin. Beyond his rooms was the library and it was here that Altair's parents had invested their money to help fund research. The money was used to buy books for the astronomical and astrophysics wing, the subjects after Altair's own heart. As a center for sports and music there was no equal and Altair loved to boast of it to his friends from other schools. He regarded his teachers as being of little help or consequence except for Mr. Pond, the English and literature teacher, whose interest in Altair led to him many years later publishing his first best seller.

Altair was more concerned with his path between magic and the stars, as well as playing rugby on Saturdays, flute on Tuesdays and tennis with his father at every other opportunity. Rugby, he loved for its speed as Altair could run as fast as the wind and became the top try scorer in that year's competition. Flute he loved for the smell of his teacher's perfume and because every flute player seemed to be a girl. Tennis, well both his dad and mum had been tennis champions, so it seemed only proper to continue their legacy. As for magic and the stars, he had to let those come to him in their own time and way. And so, they did. Because after DJ came Blessing.

Altair was searching for the garden of Eden one day, the perfect place to write songs of the soul. He liked nothing better than frolicking in nature through gardens and roses and sweet spring flowers. In many ways he was a true poet. He loved the call of the wild, to get lost in the call, to let the caller and the called disappear. This was true surrender to the powers of creation within. And who better to do it with than Blessing. She was an exquisite elfin creature that his best friend had introduced him to at a party and whom for the rest of the summer he would spend every hour with, climbing hills together to seek splendor and weaving pussy willow through each other's hair. They loved racing each other through fields of long grass where the paspalum stuck to their clothes. They would pick them off afterwards one by delicious one, and dance together through the night.

Altair was unaware that beneath the surface of his world the politics of fear were stirring, because he was enveloped by the innocence and charm of love at play in his heart.

Altair faced three enemies in his battle for a path between the stars and magic. The first was the bullies. On certain occasions, for example, Reg, whom he had infuriated in Grade 6 for revealing who had actually thrown a rock through the Headmaster's window when the whole school was about to get punished, would chase him round and round the paddocks and fields of the outer school with a promise to beat Altair up if he caught him. He never did. Reg was big and heavy and used to beating up kids which was not a habit Altair wished to encourage, least of all when that punishment was directed at him. He was grateful to Reg however, as he learned how to run very fast, and build incredible stamina, two factors which helped him compete in the Sky City athletics competitions at a very high level. Altair was not unused to bullies. At elementary school an undertaker's son named Percy helped build his initial speed by chasing him around and around the elementary school opposite his house, merely for the fun and games of it. Altair was also grateful to Percy, because in one of those circuits he met his first girlfriend, Liane, from Canada Ontario, who was also a speedster and accompanied him on one of his escape routes and then on their first date which was to race each other to her home. Percy's bullying days ended when one of the nuns caught him terrorizing the kids and held his head underwater when the class next went swimming until he promised to stop his errant ways. Such were the old ways of discipline. Force met with force.

The next enemy Altair could not outrun. They were the Brotherhood, earthly agents of the dark, whom he called the Inquisitors. Altair was forced to attend classes he often loathed, and as good fortune would have it, because he was bright, he was put on individualized programs in which he taught himself, and so had little if anything to do with the Inquisitors except on exam day. Inquisitors were known for their particularly cruel methods of punishment for children. Of course, there was the strap, the cane, and the wallop, during which the Master of Discipline would force you to bend over and then hit your bottom with such force you would collide with the opposite wall and bang your head. Altair received one of these for whispering to his friend in assembly that the Master actually did do this heinous act, because no one ever saw him do it, there were no hidden video cameras or iPhones and everyone was too scared to say. But there were equally devious and manipulative methods of control used by other Masters. One Master was known for his big ears. If you spoke in his class he would come and drag you out by the ear and then yank and pull vigorously on your ear with such force that your ears would ring, you would get a headache and you would have to promise not to do it again. There was also the notorious Golden Ruler. This was used by a Master who wielded a particularly hard ruler in such a way that if you were not paying attention he would come and force you to lay your hand on the desk and rap your knuckles so hard that bruises would come, and he would watch until tears came. The Inquisitors were masters of torture, sadistic and twisted and unfortunately there were far too many of them for one kid to deal with. The exact opposite was a mild-mannered Master who was famous for having absolutely zero control of any class and so the class did what they wanted for the entire year of Grade 9 and learned exactly nothing. Altair's class used to fly paper airplanes and launch innumerable objects, a hobby the Master grew so tired of that one day he said to everyone, "OK, if you want to fight, go ahead and fight, outside!" So, the class did, and they all went outside and had a ding-dong fight and one of the bullies, Butch, ganged up with his mates against the friend that Altair was coaching in maths, Michael, laid into him and broke his arm. That was the last day Altair ever saw the mild-mannered Master.

The most difficult enemy to deal with was the dark itself sent to plunder human consciousness through the forces of fear and ignorance and innumerable distractions. The demons from the dark tried to invade Altair's world through Jean who had been besieged by demons since birth, and Manon who had attracted a demon onto her property so that it lurked around her house. Then there was Lisbeth, who unfortunately had built her house near a graveyard and incurred the wrath of local spirits who became increasingly angry and moved and smashed objects in her house. All these Altair could help by using the same words Jesus had given him to cast out demons and liberate spirits. In the case of the warriors, as it had been an ancient battlefield, he went and had a chat and they compromised. Lisbeth moved to a new house and the warriors never disturbed anyone again. Such was Altair's life and he would never wish for another as his life was far too interesting and unexpected and filled with adventure and love and mystery.

Then his elfin princess Blessing vanished.

It happened after a summer holiday in which everything was sheer delight and perfection. The flowers could not have been rosier, and the beach could not have been more romantic. The hills were rolling and alive and the grasses they cavorted in were surely planted for them alone to hide in and kiss and share secrets. As with all holidays and young lovers the joy also had to include going to school and keeping in touch and promising to return every holiday as they lived in different islands and so they parted with every good intention. And Altair sent her love letters every day.

With none in return.

First there was disbelief, then disappointment, then grief. It was like an arm or a leg had been cut off. A part of his life snatched away. And his heart hurt so badly. He was like a ship with no anchor or an adventurer with no compass. Stars and magic no longer seemed to have quite the same allure.

Days went by with no love or stars or magic. Until the visit.

Altair had been deeply devoted all this time to alchemy on the one hand and meditation and yoga on the other. He would get up every morning to practice for 2 hours and the same in the evening. He used the family's second lounge, would shut himself away with their two cats, Milligan and Ziggy, who would curl up, one at his feet and one on his lap, and away he would go, deep into worlds beyond this one. He found that by following Yogananda's instructions exactly, all the experiences of the Masters would manifest just as Yogananda had said, and at the same time, while following the practices of alchemy to the letter, equally wondrous worlds would be revealed in his consciousness for him to explore.

He could hardly have expected what came next.

One thing that Altair noticed as he deepened his practice was that ideas began to manifest in reality. Dreams would come true. He would think about someone and they would call. He would dream about a package arriving with a particular gift and a few days later it would appear unexpectedly in the post. Very simple things. Nothing to boast about. Everyone has these. But the frequency was increasing.

Meditations were the same, ever deeper and richer. Altair wrote in his diary.

'Diary of A Yogi'

"They begin like any normal meditation, deluged by disobedient thoughts and rebellious ideas. A stormy mind with a spirit as wild and free as a young horse. Then calmness, as if the ocean waves subsided all at once and a vast presence, radiant and alive, was lapping at my consciousness. Then the breath, unceasing and endless, would stop and would be drawn out of my lungs and another breath would take its place, one in which I was not the breather. My sense of self would move outwards, into the room, the street, the world and the stars, so that the people and the stars moved as one with my consciousness. I could see the phenomenal whirling of the planets and fiery spheres as well as feel them all melting into one luminous sea. Joy would fill my soul, and continue unabated until I would drag my consciousness back to this mortal coil. God as bliss, God as light, God as love, these were realities within the infiniteness of my being. Worlds upon worlds throughout the cosmos were at play within my being. The heavenly realm was made manifest in my heart. The nectar of immortality, amrita, also known as the drink of the gods, flowed through my veins. The voice of God resounded as Om throughout, just as I had heard when I was a two-year-old child. To have an experience of cosmic consciousness like this was a priceless gift, and my heart would swell with deepest gratitude. I could see how the sacred breath and mindfulness were the key to calming the ocean and how the perception of the One Light in the Shared Heart arose from this. As I dipped into silence daily, with my guru Yogananda filling my heart with the light of God, deep devotion or *bhakti* and regular yoga practice had prepared my mind and heart for omnipresence. The force of God attracted me like a bee to honey."

After these meditations Altair would go immediately to bed and sleep deeply. On this one particular night he awoke with a sudden start. A bright light filled the room. There standing in front of Altair was Yogananda. Tears filled Altair's eyes.

"Master," was all Altair could muster.

"It is time to make a choice," said Yogananda, looking straight at Altair. "You have been following the path of meditation and alchemy. In order to go deeper you need to choose only one." Then he gave Altair a most magnanimous smile and disappeared.

In the morning Altair took the winding path beside the *pohutukawa* tree to Hannah's door. He hoped she would understand.

The door opened as he stood on the top step wondering just how he should say it.

Hannah's beautiful face was framed in the doorway.

"I thought it might be you," she said.

"I had a vision." Altair's heart was beating. "Yogananda came to me. He said I could only choose one path. I need to follow him. I … I have to stop. The lessons. The alchemy."

Hannah smiled that beneficent smile Altair loved so much. She always made him feel warm no matter the occasion.

"I thought it might come to that," she said. "Some are more suited to this way and some more suited to that. You have always struck me as a Yogi."

Altair nodded not sure what else he could say.

"You may find you will come back to it, in time," said Hannah. "All that you have ever wanted, or looked for, is here now."

As Sri Yukteswar, Yogananda's guru, said to him, "Outward longings drive us from the Eden within; they offer false pleasures which only impersonate soul-happiness. The lost paradise is quickly regained through divine meditation. As God is unanticipatory ever-newness, we never tire of Him. Can we be surfeited with bliss, delightfully varied throughout eternity?"

CHAPTER 4

Koya-san

"Altair, come on," said Mary. "Is everything packed?"

His mother always got nervous when Altair went away anywhere and this, being his first overseas trip, made her more nervous than normal.

Altair's possessions were minimal. He had a credo which was to go from place to place with as little as possible. The last place he gave away everything he had except his guitar. All he had to do was pick up his pack and he was ready.

Very Zen.

The first thing he was going to do when he landed in Japan was visit the Zen temple in Shikoku he had written to asking if he could be accepted for *zazen*, or formal Zen meditation training.

It took a long time to find it. The temple was nestled in the heart of a rural area, hidden from prying eyes by an ancient forest. The Master lived in the temple itself and sent a junior monk ahead to meet Altair at the train station.

The young monk served green tea while they were waiting and then knelt in *seiza* style, the traditional formal way of sitting in Japan. Presently the Master arrived, a squat, powerfully built man who looked at them both intensely and then knelt in *seiza* style for a long time opposite Altair before speaking.

The junior monk translated as the Master spoke.

"Stay as long as you like. Follow the rules."

He then stood, bowed and left.

Altair was taken aback.

He had been expecting a little more since he had no idea exactly what "the rules" were.

The young monk, whose name was Atsushi, explained.

"Whenever you sit, sit intently. Keep your mind here now. That is Zen."

Altair nodded. He had studied Zen at university.

"You start tomorrow. 6am start. 7:15 breakfast. Then continue. If your mind is distracted the Master will hit you with a stick."

"Hit me? How hard?"

Atsushi laughed. "Hard enough to wake you up."

"How long have you been here?"

"One year."

"How many times did you get hit in the beginning?"

"Many."

"How about now?"

"Less than many."

"I see. Is there anything else I should know?"

"Stay fresh. Live freely. Like a cloud floating in the sky."

"A cloud."

"Every encounter is precious. Cherish them. There are no shortcuts."

"I am on a path of stars and magic. Is there any more you can tell me about them?"

The young monk looked closely at Altair for a moment.

"Cherish them too." He smiled, stood up, bowed like the Master and gestured for Altair to follow.

Altair sipped his tea a few minutes later alone in his room. There was little to distinguish it, *tatami* floor, rice paper walls with little decoration, a rolled-up *futon* at one end and the small table he was sitting beside.

Altair had so many thoughts flooding his head. There were all kinds of things going on beneath his mind such as the vision that had led him here in the first place. It had manifested in his first year of Chinese philosophy at University and it changed his path forever.

He was sitting in a lecture studying Zen with Dr. Tzu and gazing out the window at the sun dappling on the venetian blinds.

Suddenly he was transported, to an ancient time and past.

He was on the slopes of Tiantai Shan mountain with Master Huang Po. They were on a journey to the summit of the mountain and had stopped beside a waterfall and stream, a signpost on their spiritual pilgrimage.

The temple was gloriously surrounded by waterfalls, one of them the Flying Waterfall. The stone bridge that stretched across it, in some places only 10 inches across, was their meditation walk. The temple sat sprawling over the rocks at the top of the waterfall.

The Master said to him, "All the Buddhas and all sentient beings are nothing but the One Mind, beside which nothing exists. The Mind is without beginning and end, is unborn and indestructible. Sentient beings are attached to form and so seek externally for the Buddha. By their very seeking they lose it, for that is using the Buddha to seek for the Buddha. Stop all your conceptual thought, cease all worrying and the Buddha will appear before you."

Then the vision vanished, and Altair was staring at the blinds and sun peeking through. Dr. Tzu was speaking to him, calling his name.

"Sorry Dr. Tzu," said Altair. "I was transported." He began to describe exactly what he had seen.

"Tiantai Shan, the mountain," said Dr. Tzu. "That is what you saw. Fangguang Temple and the Shiliang Flying Waterfall. Have you been there?"

Altair shook his head.

"Then you must go," she said. "It's quite likely you were a student of Huang Po's. You have such a versatility with Zen. Have you ever thought about a scholarship in China to study Chinese philosophy? I can nominate you!"

And so, she did. With Japan the first port of call on the path between magic and the stars to explore Zen, this particular temple was dedicated to the Goddess Kannon-Guan Yin and was one of a pilgrimage of 88 temples in Shikoku. It was a special recommendation of the Professor's.

After 3 days at the temple sitting staring into a wall for 8 hours a day and getting hit with a *Keisaku* or awakening stick every time his awareness faltered, Altair had a dream. In the dream he was led by a man chanting a mantra over and over into the forests and mountains of Shikoku. He asked to talk to the Master with Atsushi.

"I wondered why you were sent to us," said the Master. "I know of your vision of Tiantai." Atsushi smiled at this. Altair had mentioned it to him after breakfast one morning as most of their day was spent in silence. "Now I know. I am merely to be a messenger for you. Take this contact. It is a Master in Koya-san, a Shingon Buddhist monastery and temple complex in Wakayama. I have contacted him already. The man in your dream was Kukai, founder of the Koya-san community. Your path continues there. You will leave tonight and arrive tomorrow morning at first light. I have arranged for rooms to be ready on your arrival. There is a retreat this weekend which you will attend."

Altair thanked him profusely and bowed low. The Master returned the bow.

"Two things," said the Master. "Firstly, Kukai will help you on your path towards magic. Things are not always what they seem. Secondly, Koya-san will help you understand the stars a little better. We are all made of the stuff of stars. When the mind is still and silent the stuff of the stars, light, can be directly realized. This is enlightenment, bright and spotless as the void, having no appearance or form whatsoever. Awaken to the One Mind and there is no enlightenment to be attained. It is within you already. The stuff of the stars, the cosmos, the One Mind, Buddha, has never ever been anywhere else."

Arriving at the train station at Koya-san there was a different smell in the air, as if the spirits were wild and free here, and the mists filled with mysteries of the mountain. Altair stared around him for signs of life, the town and streets bare at this early hour. Directly ahead lay the mountain, with the little town below it. Wooden houses with ornate tiled roofs, a temple bell ringing out for prayers, and a solitary crow cawing in response. The smell of incense was mixed in with the early morning food smells from a concealed alley as well as cedar and pine and something else, cold and wild. The blanket of secrets that was the mystical Koya-san. Altair followed the directions on the map he'd been given, while making his way up the mountain to the temple lodgings which catered for foreigners. Squirrels darted in and out of the trees, showing impish faces before dashing off to gather more acorns. There was little wind in the mists, which was fortunate as it was bitterly cold, and every step seemed to make Altair's clothing thinner until his body started shivering.

On the path the wind was calm as Altair moved up towards the Danjo Garan temple complex which marked the heart of the Mt. Koya settlement. He knew that secret Shingon Buddhist training had been taking place here for hundreds of years. He began to feel unsteady from the lack of rest as he had been on the go since yesterday. He stopped at a bend in the pathway beside a bamboo grove and settled back on his haunches for a breather. All the sounds died away completely and there was an ominous silence and then suddenly there were voices rumbling, shouts, rocks were thrown, and a hand was pulling at his own.

"Come on, Ah-chan!"

He hesitated, scrambling for his pack, which he now could not locate anywhere.

"It's me, Ren!" The voice was more urgent now. "We've got to get out of here!"

A young Japanese woman, about the same age as him, was glaring at him with impatience.

Altair didn't try to argue as a crude missile whizzed past his head and embedded itself in one of the walls at his back. He was squatting at some sort of intersection around which a crowd was gathering and throwing insults at each other as well as anything they could lay their hands on.

Altair ran as fast as his legs would carry him in the direction the girl was tugging. She didn't so much as glance behind and ran with a sure, practiced gait he could easily match.

They wove through a number of alleys and backstreets until they came to a wide-open place where a temple was under construction. There were six other lodgings surrounding it which by the looks of the numbers of people gathered outside must have catered for visiting pilgrims. In the middle of it all stood a monk in robes with a beaming smile, intense, benevolent eyes and an aura of calm. As he watched the building's progress he was chanting under his breath and referring to a map he held in his hands as he gesticulated this way and that like a conductor.

"Gyoki-san, sorry we are late. We ran into trouble," said Ren.

"So I heard," said Gyoki. "The government has not taken kindly to our extending a helping hand to the poor. They see us as a threat to stability. Taking from the rich to give to the poor. They are persecuting us whenever they can find us alone. That rock throwing welcoming committee was organized by none other than the Kansai Office of Priestly Affairs who see me as a renegade and a rebel. My only goal is to teach people about Buddhism while building temples like this that function as community centers. From here we can provide irrigation to the surrounding fields."

"But won't they attack us here?"

"Ah-chan, it is far too public, and the poor farmers would rise up in revolt. They don't want that. They hope to unsettle us and pick us off one by one, exposing our weaknesses, uncertainties and vulnerabilities and making us look foolish in the eyes of the local people. Luckily I have devoted followers like you and Ren to help me."

"It is the Bodhisattva work," said Ren with a contented sigh. "It is what drew me to you from the beginning."

"Meeting all sentient beings in streets and intersections. Teaching and transforming all regardless of means or philosophy."

"Magic and the stars," said Altair.

Ren glared at him.

"We are endowed with wonder-working power and miraculous transformations," said Gyoki, "so in that sense you are right. It is like magic to the common people. You are both learned in song, dance, music and narratives, the best way to reach the heart of these farmers. You enchant them to hope for more and reach for the stars."

Gyoki came across and took Altair and Ren's hands in his. Energy vibrated through Altair's arms, into his heart and down his legs into the soles of his feet which tingled crazily as they connected with the earth.

"I have a surprise for you both. Kukai-san will visit us here soon to pray for the farmers to be free from natural disasters and sickness. You will both meet him personally."

He looked at Altair with a twinkle in his eye.

"To help the poor, the women and children of this world, you need to find magic in the simple things, songs and symbols, dance and stories, enchantments of the heart. Perhaps one day you two will meet again in this place in another life and learn how to bring this same magic in stories and song to the entire world."

Altair was speechless. Ren closed her eyes and stayed very still as if in deep prayer and then bowed very low. Altair followed suit.

When he raised his head, his heart was thumping hard and a presence of great power, both beyond human and very deeply human, seemed to surround him in the mists. He was back at Koya-san, his pack on his back, his body pointing in the direction of the temple complex again, shivering as if to shake the earth with a coldness that was almost overpowering.

It didn't take Altair long to find his accommodation. The lodgings were in the east wing of the temple looking out over a valley and a forest. The woman who met him in the *genkan* or entryway was expecting him and was very polite. She showed him to his room which was extremely quiet and apart from those on retreat with him, who were mostly Japanese, Altair saw very few other foreigners. The retreat was conducted in total silence and at the end he was bursting to share with someone, but his Japanese language ability was too limited. On the way back to his room he passed a woman in dark sunglasses with a shaved head. She claimed she was German but looked more Indian and introduced herself as Shanti. He wasn't sure what to make of her as she looked at him intensely with bright sparkling eyes.

"I understand you are a reader," she said, to his great surprise as there was no way she could have known anything about him.

"Yes," said Altair hesitantly, "I love books …"

"No, no," she said with a laugh, "I meant a purveyor of the stars. A reader. A journeyer."

This surprised Altair even more.

"I understand you see the stars like magic."

Altair had never thought of it that way, so he simply nodded.

Suddenly he plucked up courage.

"Would you like to see how I do it?"

"I would like that very much."

They had reached his room and it seemed only natural to invite her in, so he did. There were no chairs, so she sat on the *tatami* mat. He shuffled inside his pack and pulled out an old manuscript which he placed in front of her. He made tea which he poured and then sat down with her like two conspirators over a treasure map.

She didn't look at the manuscript but merely said, "Ephemeris, and an old one at that. For astronomy and celestial navigation."

"Yes," said Altair, "Hannah, my friend, gave it to me before I left for Japan. I've been studying it."

"Do you know how to interpret it?"

"Yes, well, er, no, I kind of just feel it, like energy patterns."

"Do you know anything about Vedic or Hindu astrology?"

"No."

"Well, you will, and a lot, one day. You are a moon seer."

"How can you tell?" Altair was perplexed by Shanti.

"We are made of the stuff of stars," said Shanti. "We navigate by the stars and astrology was the original science devised by ancients in order to understand the structure and movement of the universe. Spiritual cultures like Egypt, Babylonia, India, China and Mexico were founded on the cornerstone of astrology. Even social systems derived from it as in the rule of sun and moon kings and queens. Our birth chart is a mirror of our soul and its particular incarnation. It gives us the keys to the inner unfoldment of spirit."

Shanti picked up the manuscript.

"So how do you read the energy patterns without a book or teacher to help you?"

"When I make my mind still by breathing in the central spine like Yogananda taught me then patterns become clear in my mind like a matrix. They look like energy grids, sparkling paths of the soul which appear like pictures connecting one to another in my mind."

"Could I ask you to read mine?"

"What would you like to know?" asked Altair.

"Ask what I am supposed to be doing in this life, now, right at this moment?"

Altair found the page in the manuscript corresponding to the birth date that Shanti gave him. He knew he would not be able to see her rising sign immediately so just focused on the planets in the signs and let his mind go still. He closed his eyes and relaxed. Instantly a wheel, turning slowly, came into his mind's eye as if he was seeing into a miniature picture of the cosmos when Shanti was born through a circular window. The stars and the planets formed a complicated pattern that slowly took shape like a mandala with light, color and sound. Altair watched it closely until it settled, and he could see the configurations.

Altair looked closely at Shanti. It was as if both of them were caught in a trance.

"You are a healer and an artist, a dancer. You wanted to have children but couldn't. Your totem is an elephant and you practice yoga daily, especially pranayama. Someone close to you has just died which is why you are here. You are a leader and will receive an inheritance on return. You are writing a book which is what you are supposed to be doing right now."

"How did you know?"

"The way I see it, the planets are relay stations for the reception and transmission of stellar energies. They bring to us the forces of the cosmos itself. I see planets in particular positions when you were born as portals and open myself up to the energy of those portals in their signs, where the signs are like rulers of cosmic forces that originate from the stars. These forces determine the nature of the time in which we live and because we are so focused on the personal events in our lives we miss the great powers altogether. Like hungry fish pursuing prey, we are not deeply aware of the ocean or its current and flow. All I shared with you is what I see when I open up the portals and read the symbols as they flow through by tuning into the current of the ocean."

"Thank you," said Shanti, "for where I am now that was unbelievably accurate."

Instead of leaving Shanti stayed sitting and pondering. Then she said, "Can I ask you for one more thing?"

Altair nodded.

"Today I went for a Shingon initiation. I don't know why, I can't explain it, I just went and did it. Can you tell me what you see? You may be able to shed some light on my true name and the path I am meant to follow."

"No problem," said Altair with a touch too much bravado as he felt the flow of cosmic forces enter him. It was easier now, as he had found before when he did a series of readings for his friends all in a row. Strange things somehow just manifested.

"I can see you already," grinned Altair as if he was watching a movie. "You are in a line with many others. Blindfolded. A monk is giving you a flower to hold. You are being led to a mandala. It is shaped like a …"

Altair hesitated before continuing. "A Diamond …"

"The Diamond Realm," confirmed Shanti.

"The Diamond Realm," repeated Altair as if he were singing a refrain in a song with her.

"The flower is landing on a figure, a Buddha, the one you have the deepest karmic connection with, a woman, with 1000 arms," continued Altair.

"Senju Kannon," said Shanti with a sigh. "Avalokiteshvara Guan Yin."

Altair looked at her expectantly.

"Remarkable," said Shanti, "I couldn't hope for better confirmation. Do you know who you are?"

"*Watashi wa jinsei ni tsuite benkyou shite imasu*," said Altair.

"A student studying on the path of life," said Shanti, translating the Japanese. "And a *Naga*."

"*Naga*?" It was the first time Altair had heard this name.

"I have met only one before. A woman. An energy worker like you. In Canada. She could read a person's body and diagnose them for all manner of ailments. A *Naga* is a manifestation of some aspect of the cosmos. Enormous responsibility and significant powers or siddhis come along with being a *Naga* so you must be tremendously careful. It will appear you do magic to other human beings. Patanjali was thought to be a manifestation of the *Naga* of eternity. *Naga* is an ancient energy so guard it well. A *Naga* can cross the place between worlds with remarkable ease and hear immortal whisperings in the ether. You are incredibly innocent, almost naive, so be careful who you trust and help. You will make many mistakes I am sure but that is all part of the path and must be cherished."

Shanti reached into her pocket and took out a tiny charm.

"This is for you. Keep it safe."

"I will," said Altair and looking closely he saw the woman he had seen in his vision, Guan Yin, embossed in gold in a tiny oval locket. "Thank you."

He slid it into the manuscript.

Shanti got up and went to the door. She turned one last time and bowed low with a look of deep serenity written across her face.

"Where are you off to next?" said Shanti. "India?"

"China," said Altair, "on a scholarship."

"I think not," said Shanti, with a most bemused expression on her face. Then she quickly gathered herself. "Sorry, I have no idea why I said that. I just have a hunch. I hope you find success with whatever you do."

CHAPTER 5

Kailash

When he returned to his room Altair thought about consulting the ephemeris for himself, but this had never served him well. It always triggered events but never in a way he could foresee. So it was now. Shanti's fateful words were somehow deeply woven into the fabric of time, as within a few minutes he received a call from the temple hostess to say he had a message to call the Chinese Embassy. He wondered whether he should call back immediately and following a hunch he decided to wait and telephone his mother Mary a little later. Perhaps she already knew the results of the scholarship to China.

    He lay on his bed pondering the fires that had ignited within him, the desire to travel across China and study the Taoist philosopher Chuang Tzu and the now very new and burning desire, a yearning to travel to Tibet and India and learn from the Siddha Masters. He felt intensely human, as if the stillness of the Shingon Temple was calling to him, and that maybe the continual grind of an academic life was not as attractive as the flow of study with a Master such as Yogananda or the Dalai Lama. It wasn't long before he fell asleep, dreaming of a monk crossing a very different bridge, a bridge across forever that connected worlds way beyond this one.

He awoke suddenly to the voice of his mother. He had no idea what time it was.

"Altair is that you?"

Speakerphone.

"Mmm," Altair was still half asleep.

"Altair, the Chinese Embassy rang."

Mary hesitated.

"You didn't get the scholarship. They gave it to an American scholar already at the University in China. Professor Tzu herself rang to confirm. You were in second place. So, if it falls through …"

"Mum, I'm going to India …"

"There's one more thing. I'm so sorry about the scholarship."

"I'm not, because I've decided to go to …"

"A telegram arrived this morning …"

"India! I'm going to go to …"

"Yes! From India, the telegram is from India! How did you know?"

"What?"

"Do you remember you asked to visit that Foundation, the Krishnamurti group in Varanasi?"

"The Krishnamurti …?"

Sleep was getting the better of him. Altair was sure he was hearing things, getting the messages all muddled up.

"Yes, they've sent you an invitation."

There was a faint light now in the temple room that gave the whole episode more than an edge of mystery. Altair longed to be on the plane right now. India? An invitation? It all seemed too good to be true.

He stood up and walked over to the speakerphone.

"Mum, that's great, that's just great."

"I'm so happy for you darling."

"So am I. I'll call you back later when I'm more awake."

Altair walked out into the corridor and headed towards the entrance to the temple. It was just before sunrise as he stepped out.

He decided to go on the long walk to Okunoin, Kukai's mausoleum and Japan's largest cemetery. In the early morning mists, it was the perfect place to clear his head. According to Shingon Buddhism belief there are no dead there, only waiting spirits. Kukai, also known as Kobo Daishi, came out of meditation there upon the arrival of Miroku or Maitreya, the Buddha of the Future in his visions.

As Altair crossed the Ichi No Hashi Bridge, reaching the outskirts of the first headstones, it was like he was crossing a bridge between two worlds, as something strange was happening in the mists. He thought it was the early morning winds, moving and trembling but something else was stirring. Dizzying cedars dotted the graves, hiding the sky. The atmosphere was different, the air charged with the sacred.

"Kukai!"

A figure was forming in the mists, like a ghost. Altair's surprise was so strong he had to check his feet, that they were still connected to the ground.

The vision filled the forest. It began to spill out beyond the corners as if delicate fingers of light were searching and trembling for something. Kukai was holding a dragon blossom, coming into bloom, and the mists looked like the ocean rising, both signs of the future Buddha, Maitreya. Kukai was as transparent as fragile silk and shimmered like delicately disturbed water on a calm lake. Altair felt deeply moved. It was as profound as any dream or vision he had ever experienced. The beauty of the sacred, and its holiness touched his eyes with tears. As Altair watched, the vision became a portal, just like when he read someone's astrology chart, and he was transported beyond the confines of the cemetery and the mountain he was standing upon, into another mountain range, one with its own mists and dreams and visions, as if he was looking across a vast natural vista and into another universe.

Altair was gifted with a mystical vision of the future, seated on the top of Mt Kailash on an outspread mandala. Shiva and Parvati, turned to look at him, then blended into Saraswati and Brahma. The fusion was deep, immersed in the ecstatic bliss of creation. Then they in turn blended into the wisdom and knowledge of the Bodhisattva Manjushri and the Goddess Benzaiten Saraswati. The fierce sun, the soft snow, the blue skies, the mystic mists, made the journey of the Tibetan pilgrims circumambulating the mountain below look even more arduous. In the light he saw himself, now at some period in the future, making his way up a mountain range with a group of people, traversing the Himalayas.

Shanti was right after all.
It was India, not China.
Something deeper had called Altair, perhaps the wild of the Himalayas.

"Boarding for Kathmandu at Gate 22!" came the call over the loudspeakers at Bangkok Airport. Altair had been staying with a friend of his, Ting, at a monastery in Northern Thailand after flying out from Japan and Koya-san.
"You should follow your dreams," she said.
So, he did.
He decided to follow the dream of Tibet and Samye Monastery, by going overland through Nepal.
He was ready to get underway to Nepal and had been itching to do so ever since landing in Thailand, but he'd promised Ting a visit and it was a good opportunity to weigh up the paths ahead once he was unable to take up the scholarship in China. Some dreams weighed more heavily than others. Even in airport terminals.

"Excuse me Sir?" It was a gentleman in fine clothes with gold trim, gold-rimmed sunglasses and a very tanned bald head. "Could you lend me a hand?"

He turned around behind him to lift the largest teddy bear Altair had ever seen.

"Do you have much check-in luggage? I am wondering if I could bother you to take this?"

Altair nodded dumbly. He seemed to remember somewhere his mother warning him about the Asian drugs trade and Bangkok being a kingpin in the drug triangle.

Naively he took the bear, which was as large as he was, and lifted it clumsily into the plane, to the wide-eyed glances of the hostesses.

Soon they were skywards and heading towards Nepal. The flight and the landing were smooth and the tender bump on the runway filled Altair's eyes with tears although he could have never said why. It was like he was coming home.

He clambered off, hugging the bear and made his way to immigration, looking out for the bear's owner. There was no sign. Altair felt anxious. He could have sworn the gentleman had got off the plane with him, though he didn't see him sitting in economy class. Suddenly there was a tug on his shirt. It was an officer in a military uniform. Altair's heart skipped a beat. But his consternation was met with a smile.

"This way Sir, please."

The officer opened a door he hadn't noticed to the side of immigration.

It was semi-dark, a long smooth corridor with no distinguishing features or signs.

The next moment he emerged to a fanfare of trumpets and a crowd surging towards him as he marched with the bear down between a guard of honour, to join the bear's owner and another man in a wheelchair with a bandage wrapped tightly around his head.

"Welcome to Nepal!" said the man with the gold-rimmed sunglasses. That bear belongs to this man's son."

"What happened to him?" whispered Altair.

"This man is the King's brother and I am his Secretary. He was shot and wounded in an assassination attempt a few months ago.

We have just returned from America where he was taken for surgery. We are very grateful to you for helping us. We want to repay your kindness. Tell us anything you want or need in Nepal and we will make sure it is done."

Altair was given a King's feast, a luxurious hotel, as well as a Royal Tour of Nepal and its surrounding schools and educational foundations, which is how he thought this gift would serve his mission here on earth the best.

"Namaste."

A young woman seated with a small group of hikers greeted Altair in Pokhara. He was at the start of the Annapurna Circuit which snakes through lush rice paddy valleys, roaring rivers, Tibetan Buddhist villages, Hindu temples and unassailable arid Himalayan peaks. He had taken some crazy bus rides to get here after the tours of Nepalese schools, on overloaded buses with 20 seats and 40 people to pack in like sardines. He had ridden on the rooftops of buses along insanely dangerous ravines where the slightest mistake would have meant a fatal fall of several hundred meters to their death. He had even driven into Tibet with a truckload of Chinese soldiers which left him feeling completely ill at ease even though they had been very civil and shared their Chinese superfood biscuit rations with him.

With his pack on his back and his heart beating with excitement, Altair was ready for the first ascent, which he was told would climb to giddy heights of several thousand meters and leave him breathless and with aching muscles especially around his kneecaps.

It was with a measure of relief that he met the woman's smile and greeting.

"Namaste."
"Monica."
"Altair."
"Climbing alone?"
Altair nodded.
"Want to join us?"

Altair smiled again. As simple as that and he was one of them. He soon discovered they were all ballet dancers from Belgium. Monica was the leader, and she had gathered her friends, Cecilia, Irene, Louise and Peter, to come on the hike with her. Together they made their way through lush hills and over swollen rivers, in and out of bamboo forests and traversing waterfalls. Sometimes they skipped across rocks and at other times the trail wove into and up hillsides, with giant blocks at some parts which went upwards for hours leaving them all with sore knees at each resting point. Each night they stayed at a different village along the trail in very basic teahouse accommodation. Mattresses varied from very sparse to somewhat thicker, walls would often have cracks to encourage a view, showers ran from cold to very cold and toilets smelt bad or just plain intolerable. Food was usually dahl, rice, lentils, potatoes and tea. As their bodies adjusted so did the path, from muddy tracks to dusty paths with valleys revealing the snowy mountain peaks from time to time.

"Tashi Delek."

In the light of one early morning high up in the Annapurna mountain range they were met by a young Tibetan monk smiling broadly and sipping tea. His saffron robes flapped in the breeze.

"You teach us?"

Altair felt a chill up his back. He knew this young monk would help him connect to his dream as a child, that this boy would somehow link him to Samye.

"I ... I'll ..." he had trouble getting his words out.

It was Monica, the lead dancer in the Belgian ballet group who replied.

"We dance," she said, "we love dancing!" And she turned and twirled and did a dainty pirouette right there on the spot.

The monk clapped in delight and called out something in Tibetan. Instantly doors opened all around the group and young monks and several nuns gaily skipped out to join them.

The monks were composed and free and wild all at once. Then Cecilia danced followed by Irene and Louise. The monks copied them all as Altair breakdanced and Peter showed them some jazz steps. It was a hilarious introduction. The young nuns pointed and giggled.

At the end they all bowed respectfully.

"We are happy to teach you our meditation," said the monk with a smattering of English. "Here …"

And he brought out some ancient texts all in Sanskrit that none of the group could read.

"This here," he said. "Breathing." He pointed to a diagram of a Yogi sitting. "Like this." He began to demonstrate so Altair and the dancers all sat down together to practice.

The young monk, whose name was Jampa, which means loving kindness and is the Tibetan name for the Buddha Maitreya, took great pride in showing Altair sitting postures, breathing techniques and how to visualize the various deities.

"Inside or outside?" he said pointing to their rooms which were simple dwellings built of brick.

"We'd rather stay outside," said Altair laughing as he watched a group of four monks mimicking Peter as they danced in unison across the courtyard.

"Not cold?"

They shook their heads vigorously although it was rather brisk at this high altitude.

"You," said Jampa pointing at Altair. "Who?"

"Altair," said Altair. "Shyam."

The monk nodded, gesturing wide with his arms. "Space."

"Shyam. That's right. It means space in Sanskrit."

"You monk." He tapped his chest. It was more a statement than a question.

Altair hesitated, not knowing whether to nod or shake his head, so he decided to smile instead. The other monks had gathered around, listening as Jampa chatted in Tibetan, translating the staccato English conversation.

Altair stayed with them like this, exchanging culture and dance, meditation and mindfulness all day until the sun went down, when he headed to the teahouses with the group and the monks and nuns to their own lodgings.

They were all well wrapped up and ready for the cold night air when they began drinking tea just before dinner.

After a few sips Altair hesitated.

"Anyone taste anything funny?"

"It all tastes the same to me, awful," said Monica grimacing.

"Did anyone add their iodine tablets?" said Peter.

"I did," said Altair.

"Me too," said Monica.

Irene, Louise, and Cecilia all shook their heads.

"Boiled water?" Altair asked the owner of the tea house in Nepalese.

The owner nodded.

"Can we look?"

He gestured towards the fire where there was a pot heating over logs.

"It has to be properly boiled to be effective," said Monica. "And if it isn't …"

"Then the water source could be the problem," said Altair.

"Can we see the water?" asked Altair. "Where it comes from?"

The owner nodded and took a flashlight and walked with them outside the simple shelter to the water tank around the back. High up in the mountains some of the lodgings were infamous for polluted water supplies.

Altair stood on tiptoes and looked over the edge of the water tank.

What they saw made their stomachs churn. A dead rat, some other indescribable objects and bird droppings, were floating in the water.

"I'm going to be sick," said Monica.

Altair felt his stomach clench.

"Let's go back to the hotel."

The hotel was little more than a wooden shell with some rooms.

And it was to this wooden shell that they were all confined together for the next three days, much of it spent moaning or going to the toilet to throw up or emit watery substances from either end, much to the dismay of the other members of the group who were trying to keep everything down.

Altair struggled up as often as he could to meditate and do yoga, which kept the food down rather than up, and he drank enormous quantities of purified water, much to the delight and then growing consternation of his ever-groaning stomach.

It was in one of these long nights that he saw Babaji. He could never be quite sure which night it was as he was so sick but the message Babaji gave was clear and direct.

Babaji looked straight at Altair with dark sparkling eyes. His mere presence engulfed Altair in a wave of spiritual blessing. Altair could not stand to bow at the feet of this angelic being, so he let his heart kneel in front of Babaji in humility.

Babaji was young, just like in all the pictures Altair had seen of him. Babaji had a power allowing direct telepathy between two souls so what Altair heard was like a stream of nectar flowing between two hearts.

"What do you think of the schools you have seen here?"

"I am looking for so much more sir, the blending of yoga and science, of life and literature, of love and peace."

"Child," the Master said, "the forces on earth are mixed, like sand and sugar, so be wise. Look for schools blessed by men and women of God-realization."

"Sir, the Western schools are filled with science and the Eastern with philosophy. One can benefit from the other."

"I know you are interested in the East and the West. That is why I am here. East and West must share the golden path of spirituality and activity. Your dreams and visions can shake material reality when founded in yoga science and meditation and transformed through action. Altair, very soon Krishna will visit you, and help you understand your path in the West. There are many very young Yogis waiting to be awakened. You will know by the signs I send you, the Bhagavad Gita and the Goddess Saraswati. You will write about the unity between the Christ, Krishna and the Buddha. That inspired sons and daughters of God speak with the same truth."

"Babaji, how can I undertake such a task?"

"Why do you doubt? Whose work is all this? Who is the doer behind all your actions? Who is the meditator and who dreams the dreams?"

The vision was fading. Altair bowed humbly in farewell and Babaji smiled.

"I will visit you again."

The others were roused and looked up from their beds.

"I saw something," said Monica sleepily. "A light. Did you have a visitor?"

Altair laughed and told them the story of Babaji. Irene looked at Altair curiously.

"Does this sort of thing often happen to you?"

"Only when I'm not expecting it," Altair said with a smile. "I know I have to meditate more. Then I will be able to see the Great Masters hiding behind the sunlight."

"Curiouser and curiouser," said Irene as they all laughed.

CHAPTER 6

Ketumati

Altair travelled overland alone from Nepal to India to visit the Krishnamurti group in Varanasi, also known as Benares. He sat one day in the late afternoon in the garden of Krishnamurti's own house. The group had kindly put him up in the house, complete with his own servants, and he was chatting with Krishnamurti's gardener Henry, who was an exceptionally wise man.

"Why do you think Babaji wanted me to meet Krishna?" said Altair although he hadn't the faintest idea how this could possibly happen.

"Because of your knowledge of other worlds," replied Henry.

Altair looked at Henry in surprise. "Other worlds? Like the billions of stars and planets out there with habitable life?"

Henry laughed. "No not that. You will experience those worlds directly I'm sure. In your future, rather than mine. I am too old for space travel. Not the world of ghosts and spirits either. You will be able to contact those worlds too, in time, perhaps in your homeland. No, I mean the Pure Lands like Maitreya's Ketumati where we are now, or Amitabha's Sukhavati or Guan Yin's Mount Potalaka. Masters, saints and Buddhas have known of these other worlds for thousands of years. Take Shambhala for instance. The Dalai Lama says in the Kalachakra Tantra that the Pure Land of Shambhala, which is ruled over by Maitreya, can only be visited by a worthy person. I ask myself what a worthy person is, often. Pure Lands are not really part of this universe at all. They intertwine and are woven into the fabric of this world. People like you and Krishnamurti and others who practice the portal of deep constant presence can become aware of them. And aware of the beings that inhabit them. The beings we call Buddhas and Christs, gods and goddesses, they are in all our religions as well as our myths, legends and fairy tales for a reason."

Henry stood up for a moment and gestured around the garden. "Take Ketumati for instance."

Altair blinked. He could have sworn he caught a glimpse of a completely different sort of garden, one like he first experienced as Palmo Shonu in the gardens of Zahor with Princess Mandarava. It was a garden glowing with energy, vibrant green, clear energy fields surrounding every flower, plant and tree. Any point could be a portal that would transport a person's awareness into other times or places.

"We are closer than close, closer than a heartbeat, worlds that are able to be known through stillness, silence and presence and letting go of the known," said Henry. "And love, as you will find out."

Altair touched the grass. His hand disappeared, immersed in energy.

"Yes, I see it too," said Henry, "the power of presence and cosmic consciousness. We are truly made of the same stuff as the stars. So how have you come to this awareness Altair? What has helped you along the way?"

"Firstly, my dreams of Samye. That made me very curious about life and what came before and after even at the tender young age of three years old. Secondly, the visions of Zahor and many other places, Masters and guides. They made me aware of worlds beyond our own. The third was meditation, the doorway to presence, which is like the Garden of Eden here on Earth. Meditation made me aware that paradise is located right here in the garden of our hearts.

Fourth would be action. When I was at Koya-san I decided to follow my dreams, however they turned out. I put all my faith in Divine Mother and followed the signs. Fifth and last is Kriya Yoga. My connection with Babaji through Yogananda elevated me to great heights of awareness, like climbing Mt. Kailash."

"When you breathe in such an active and sacred way as in Kriya Yoga, you actually charge the particles of your inner consciousness, a cosmos of your own creation existing within the astral spine and make the matter of this world very thin, so the portals of the chakras become much more accessible and easier to use and allow you to move between worlds to accomplish whatever your destiny and mission is. Great Masters have always known this. That is why many institutions fear it. That is why the ignorant imprison us by feeding us limited thoughts and fueling our material desires."

"Why?" said Altair.

"Think of the possibilities, if we realized just how powerful we were. It would revolutionize churches, temples and governments, schools and businesses. If we realized there was a way to bridge this world and all others. If we knew the power of love language and communication with presence."

"The key is intention," said Altair. "We only have to think it and use the power of divine imagination."

"Yes," said Henry. "It is in the interests of those who inspire fear and ignorance and limited thought to keep the rest of us thinking the only reality is what we see through our senses. The power that would be unleashed worldwide is beyond anything we can imagine now if we were all to be free. It is about the collective, unity. We are not supposed to do it alone. It is about going home together."

"So those that want to keep the wealth and power have a vested interest in keeping us imprisoned in our limited thinking?"

"Yes, those who have the most fear are holding on tight to what they have, which is in actuality very little."

"And the Masters want to open this bridge across forever?"

"Even the Masters have different perspectives on opening portals. If they open it too soon, before most people have developed awareness, they could create an imbalance in the light and dark forces at play."

"What about nature? I seem to be able to connect to snakes, dolphins, and hummingbirds." said Altair with a smile.

The Krishnamurti group was located on a native wildlife reserve in Varanasi. Though there were no dolphins or hummingbirds there were snakes and eagles.

Henry smiled. "Those may well serve you in time. They are unconcerned with our problems. In fact, we have upset their natural balance more than in any other time in history."

"How do I connect more deeply with them?"

"The same way you are connecting to the Masters. Make a clear intention. Quiet the mind, still the heart, open up to limitless possibilities and surrender."

"When will it happen?"

"Don't be so impatient! Everything has its own time."

At that very moment an eagle soared overhead and swooped down low as if feasting its eyes on the garden below.

"You see," said Henry. "They are listening. Give it time. I imagine there are many surprises in store for you."

In the wake of the eagle's path a sudden brisk wind picked up, ruffling Altair's hair.

Dark black storm clouds loomed swiftly over the horizon where there were none before.

"You'd best be getting inside," said Henry. "There's a storm brewing."

"I need to buy some yoghurt!" Altair said and stood up in a hurry. "It helps my stomach settle after curry. Do you think I'll have time?"

"Maybe," said Henry. "Better hurry!"

Altair dashed off down the path towards town. He passed by one of the fields where the boys were playing cricket.

"Six!" came a cry.

Altair turned seeking the source of the call when he received an enormous crack on the nose. He stumbled back, stunned, stars spinning in his vision.

A group of boys came running up.

"Sorry, Sir!"

"That's all right." Altair was still dazed. "I ... I'm from down south. I used to play cricket at school too."

"Oh, Sir, do you know Sachin Tendulkar? He is the God of Cricket!"

It wasn't long before they were all best of friends.

On Altair's first day at the school, he'd arrived at the office in the morning knowing they were expecting him, to find himself sitting beside an auburn-haired woman looking rather pensive, who introduced herself as Angela.

"I'm off home today," she said, "my father is ill, and they can't find a replacement. I don't want to leave them in the lurch."

"What do you teach?" said Altair.

"English, drama and music."

"I have a background in Performing Arts," said Altair. "I might be able to help."

Half an hour later he was signing papers as a substitute teacher and getting Angela to show him around. The school put him up in Krishnamurti's own house, complete with servants, which initially he felt most uncomfortable about until he discovered that it was their job and they were extremely proud of it, having served generations of famous people including Krishnamurti himself before Altair.

So now as he headed into town just before the storm, to get his yoghurt, he thought back over the incredible sequence of events that had brought him here to the holy city of Varanasi.

After Nepal and Tibet, he had stayed in New Delhi just to see the Taj Mahal. The tour he decided to take to see the famous landmark proved to be the comedy routine of his adventure so far.

"All aboard," shouted the driver as they lined up for the bus in the dust and fumes of the early morning traffic outside the youth hostel in New Delhi. "We have to be back by 5pm. Evening curfew. Hurry up!"

That was true. Delhi was in the midst of riots, and soldiers with rifles patrolled the streets and roofs looking to shoot looters.

The tourists knew that to return after 5pm was to place their lives in peril.

Everywhere they looked was a mass of dangling power cables, narrow streets, cycle rickshaws, winding old lanes leading to spice markets and traffic everywhere.

Some of the stares they got were frankly unfriendly and for a woman, Delhi could be a dangerous place, so they needed to know places to avoid, especially after dark.

Altair wore his hair long and had massive curls so from behind looked every bit like a young woman. One of those days in Delhi he had an older man with his wife saunter up beside him in the crowd and grope at his breasts. Altair felt terribly invaded and was so incensed he turned and punched the man hard on the nose. The fellow hurried away with his wife through the madding crowd.

The bus lurched away from the hostel in a pall of smoke and careered down the highway knocking two cycle rickshaws off the road and into the ditch beside them to the insults and waving fists of their drivers. The bus driver didn't seem to care at all.

The Taj Mahal is located in Agra, so they had a little way to go, some five hours or so, and a number of palaces and scenic spots to see on the way.

They came to the first stop, Agra Fort. The driver was very clear they didn't have long, as traffic had been heavy these first three hours. "We only have ten minutes so no photos," he said.

A young German couple started grumbling immediately.

"We didn't pay all this money for a ten-minute tour. He can wait."

They took their bags and cameras and set off for a stroll.

The rest of the group looked dubiously at the driver who seemed extremely nervous.

Sure enough, ten minutes later, on the dot, he climbed up into the driver's cab and shouted, "Time to go!" in the direction of the German couple who were the last to get back on. They were still atop the monumental Delhi Gate and waving buoyantly at the bus. When the driver put his foot on the gas pedal to resume his trip, minus the German couple, the tourists were all aghast. There was lots of shouting, and the Germans could still be heard yelling insults in German from the walls, as the bus pulled away from the fort.

To no avail.

The driver would not turn back, regardless of threats and cajoling, and kept his head down for the rest of the trip to the Taj Mahal.

They stopped at several other minor attractions, losing at least one passenger at each spot.

By the time they got to the Taj Mahal, they were a decimated group of tourists.

"We must be hurrying!" continued the driver, scarcely pausing at this beautiful monument for long enough to take some decent pictures. "5 o'clock, 5 o'clock!"

It was beginning to sound like the rant of a madman. By any reasonable calculations the bus should make it home just in time.

So off they went, at a giddy gait, swerving around this obstacle or that car or knocking an occasional rickshaw off the road when it wouldn't shift for the driver.

After about 2 hours they arrived at a fairly nondescript hotel, small, dingy and rather unkempt. The driver met with another man out front and they shook hands gleefully. He gestured at them all to come in.

"Tea stop, souvenirs," yelled the driver, proudly clapping the new man on the shoulder as he introduced him. "This is my uncle. My uncle's hotel," he waved his hands with aplomb as if this were the most scenic attraction they had yet feasted their eyes upon.

"We have time for a stop," he said as if to assure the group of his intentions to take good care of them finally.

Then the driver and the uncle disappeared, no doubt to discuss commissions and sales and the group were left to the extremely tardy tea service of one older gentleman, the sole waiter, server and tea pourer. Almost one hour later, the longest stop they had made anywhere, and Altair decided to go on the warpath. He found the driver laughing out the back with a group of men, smoking and drinking chai.

"The time, the time!"

The driver glanced at his watch and immediately looked like he had been hit with a club. Fear filled his face and he sprung up like a jack in a box.

"Hurry up, hurry up!" He began yelling at the top of his voice.

They piled back into the bus.

"We must be taking a shortcut," said the driver.

He put his foot on the gas pedal and belted off at a gut-wrenching pace, turning and scurrying down one winding narrow lane after another.

Soon he reached a long straight section which looked like it went on forever.

"Hold on!" he announced with more than a hint of trepidation in his voice.

The bus hurled past shops and doorways with barely a hair's breadth separating them.

It was clear this shortcut was going to put everyone at death's door if the driver had anything to do with it.

The next moment they saw looming up ahead of them a very low-lying bridge under which they would not pass.

"Hold on!" commanded the demon driver.

The bus hit the bridge with an enormous crash and a sound like bullets firing out of a cylinder could be heard as packs and bags which were on the roof-rack shot backwards off the top of the bus with the roof-rack and upper connections following in a tangle on the ground.

"Sorry! Sorry!" was all the mad driver could repeat over and over.

Altair got out slowly in a daze with the other passengers. The bus was still running, and they gathered up their possessions and placed them back on board.

The driver said very little, bar the occasional sorry, on his way back to the hostel.

Needless to say Altair and the remaining passengers arrived late, past the curfew, and had to clamber secretively on the emergency escape ladders at the back of the hotel. They clutched and scraped at windowsills, bruising their shins and fingers and cracking nails, as they forced their way into one of the back windows of the hostel, in constant fear of their lives, in case they were mistaken for looters by one of the soldiers positioned on nearby roofs.

Perhaps never again would Altair take a bus tour in India.

Altair found himself not on a bus heading to Varanasi, but on a train, firstly in the lowest class carriage which was basically the baggage train filled with cattle and chickens, bad smells and cow-dung, and old men chewing betel nuts, teeth stained reddish-black from years of chewing this addictive nut, which they spat out on the floor at his feet. After a couple of hours of olfactory torture Altair upgraded to second class which was just as crowded and had some people riding the roof. A few hours of this experience and he went to first class which meant he had a seat and finally for the last segment he allowed himself the luxury of AC or air conditioning and found himself in a cabin with 4 other men, all with the same birthday as him. September 7th. This birthday had led to a number of synchronistic events. On one bus trip in Nepal he found himself riding on the roof of a bus with three other travelers, all with this same birthday. And when he started university, he was walking up the hill to Queen Victoria Park when an old woman on the other side of the road pointed at him and called out.

"Hey you!"

She made her way across the road to him.

"You were born the same day as Queen Elizabeth the First."

It wasn't a question.

And she was right.

She proceeded to tell him many things about his life. How he would work with children in the arts, be a leader, travel to America and work as a healer.

Meetings with remarkable people in the most unlikely places never seemed out of place.

It was the same in Varanasi.

After signing up for the job, Angela took him out on a boat on the Ganges for an hour just before lunch.

The sun was high over the holy river, casting a steady glow, big and imposing in the sky. The air was filled with the aroma of sandalwood and jasmine flowers. Angela found a boatman who rowed them close to the shore, bathing them in the aftermath of the morning cremation rituals. That meant an arm that had not been burned properly by the cremation *ghats* floated by the boat. An occasional body too.

"You may not be surprised to know that I heard you were coming," said Angela. "I was hoping against hope that you would be able to fill my position. You know they are interested in you for other reasons. That is why they accepted you so easily. It's usually much more difficult to get a job here. There are many volunteers waiting in line. The principal told me you would be here this morning."

Altair had a strange feeling that the school, the Principal and Krishnamurti were all somehow tied into Babaji's prophecy of him meeting Krishna.

He found himself searching the nearby markets for some yoghurt he loved just before the storm set in.

The markets were lazy, colorful and chaotic. Old men, stray dogs and bodies close to death lay strewn across his path at every turn. Men with baskets heaped with herbs tried to sell their wares and shopkeepers tried to bargain with him. He quickly found the shop he was looking for and ordered a mango lassi while he was waiting. He listened to the chatter of the customers around him and thought of the vision Babaji and Henry had brought him. A bridge across forever that he could travel over and link other worlds and Pure Lands. He wanted to take all the women and children that were caught up in wars and strife far away from here, to set them free, with stars and magic …

Sometime in the night he awoke to the sounds of thunder and pelting rain. The servant and his family were fast asleep and the house itself was eerily serene amidst the backdrop of the boom and bang of nature's titanic forces clashing.

There was a soft knock at the door.

Altair waited. The storm rattled on.

The knock came softly again.

No one was going to answer it. The servants were still asleep. They were in the middle of a storm.

"Hello," said Altair as softly as the knock. "Who's there?" And he got up to open the door.

Standing there in the wind and rain, without an umbrella, as dry as a bone, was a woman. She was dressed in the orange cloth of a sanyasi, a wandering holy person. She had blonde hair, bright blue eyes, and was holding an ancient scroll in her hands. Behind her, in all directions, lay a tumbling sea of water that fell in ever increasing streams, pausing only now and then to catch its breath before resuming its fury, like a constant waterfall pouring straight down.

"May I come in?" Her voice was soothing, like a clear mountain stream.

Altair was at a loss for words. He gestured for her to come in and noticed that her sandals left no wet mark on the floor even though she had somehow come through the storm to get here. Now he could see her clearly for the first time. She was very young, yet wore spectacles, wore no hood or rain gear and seemed not to notice

Diary of a Yogi

nature's spectacle which had been crashing all around her. She had a simple red *bindu*, the sacred symbol for the unmanifested universe, painted between her eyebrows. She stood in the entrance like a goddess. She reminded him of Krishna himself.

"Altair?"

Altair nodded.

"I have been sent to bring you a message."

Altair could momentarily see through the veils of time and perceive the bridge across forever that Henry had spoken of, the unity linking all beliefs and faiths that Babaji had guided him to. He could feel the language of love breaking through to speak to his heart and know of the timeless awareness that awakens when you are in the presence of divinity.

The scroll had binding which the woman carefully unwrapped and then unrolled the parchment before handing it to Altair.

"This is for you. Krishna bid me give it to you."

Altair took the scroll and held it at the top and bottom so that he could see it better.

"This is Saraswati," said the woman, in a sweet sing-song voice, pointing to the Goddess who sat playing a sitar surrounded by peacocks. "You have been devoted to Her many times over many lives."

"Babaji said you would come."

She nodded and pointed to another section of the scroll, in Sanskrit.

"Chapter 12, the Bhagavad Gita. Bhagavad Shri Krishna spoke to Arjuna and said, 'Those who fix their minds on Me, who constantly glorify Me, and possess great faith, I consider them to be most perfect.' That is the message from Lord Krishna to you."

She took the scroll from Altair, rolled it up, bound it and handed it back to him.

"I think there are things I need to tell you," she said. "Altair, you were a 16th century Raj in Northern India."

The Sanyasi's voice was so sweet it lifted him above the storm.

"You were married with three wives. You governed a small kingdom in what is now Rajasthan."

Altair felt his body drifting, lifting upwards, soaring into the heavens.

"You worshipped Saraswati."

Just like Palmo Shonu with Princess Mandarava in Zahor, thought Altair.

Below him the countryside splayed out like a balloon and ahead of him a magnificent palace was sitting in all its grandeur and splendor. He was part of it and it was all around him. Great forts with round towers rose up sprawling over hills and valley plains next to rivers. Temples, houses and markets were held within its walls.

Altair saw people running in every direction, barricading doors and windows. He found himself in the midst of a large group of men, brave, armed and ready for fighting, standing before the last of seven massive gates.

Three women, dressed in beautiful saris stood at his side, all weeping.

The one closest to him, took his arm and spoke loudly and clearly to the throng.

"We are besieged sire, but should you go out to battle, and die, we will be lost without you, and surely we will not survive what is to follow."

Altair simply nodded. He felt heavy and realized he was wearing armor. One of the men was helping him get up on a horse. He was eating his last betel nut together with his troops. He donned his saffron robes which his first wife, the one that had spoken to the crowd, handed him.

"The invading army outnumbers us ten to one," said the man now in front of him brandishing a double-edged scimitar.

Altair nodded again. He knew the warrior's code. Compassion for defeated foes, generosity towards the helpless, fair play in battle, respect for women and conduct of warfare governed by elegant forms and ceremonies. His people loved him, and he was renowned for his courage on the battlefield. He was part of a proud martial tradition and he had a passion for war. Everyone was waiting for his signal.

He drew his sword, holding it aloft and cried out in a wild yell, and the gates opened on his command. The warriors on horseback circled and flew with him out the gates and onto the hills and down into the valleys. Many were mounted, and some were on foot.

They were met by a storm of shrieks and yells and blinding fury as the two armies collided. Horsemen, war elephants, soldiers with swords, lances, matchlocks and bows and arrows battled in the breach, many hurled into the air together, and many crushed by the falling debris caused by siege engines.

War elephants, as many as three hundred, joined the onslaught. One of them trampled a man near him, rolled him up in his trunk and crushed him. The elephant then turned on Altair, smashed its trunk down on his horse's back, breaking it in two with a terrible crack and throwing Altair in the air. When Altair hit the ground, he was stunned and dazed. The battle had carried him right near the center of the fighting as he struggled to his feet, now a short distance away from the invading king. The king came down from the small rise of a hill that he stood upon and faced Altair, the two men now barely meters apart. Altair was trembling like a mighty dynamo, not from fear but from grim determination. He was a warrior and to die in battle was just as honorable as to die for love. He touched his heart as he stood, thinking of his brave wives and the fate they might face if he was vanquished. Brandishing his sword, he said to himself,

"I fight for you my loves. I am a king and he is nothing."

The warriors around them continued fighting but formed a protective cordon from which no one could get in or out. The bodies piling up made a wall. Here they were, two futures, two destinies. One would continue while the other would fall.

The air seemed to grow still and silent.

Then with a roar and a shaking like two mountains clashing, the two warriors crashed into each other and fell aside, and Altair sprung up first and slashed at the other man's neck which was his most vulnerable point.

There was a clash of metal on metal as Altair's thrust missed its mark but caught the man's face and a scream split the air. The other king hurled himself in fury onto Altair pummeling him to the ground and the breath was squeezed out of him all at once by that crushing fall. Hands fixed themselves on his throat and hot bloody drops dripped down his helmet.

Altair threw himself backwards with all his might and ripped downwards, tearing away those vicious hands and swinging the sword which had been underneath him out and across.

He struck metal and then metal again as the two swords met and parried and thrust.

Then they stood apart struggling to regain their breath.

Both men were bleeding, and both were panting heavily.

Altair knew it was going badly for his men. He was their last hope and he would not fail them. He allowed himself the luxury of a single tear. His dear brave fearless wives were going to die if he did not find victory, through love and belief, in fearlessness and valor. He thought of how Krishna assured Arjuna in the Bhagavad Gita that the proper thing to do was to fight on the battlefield. He thought of his friend Mirabai and her love for Krishna which had inspired his devotion. And it was at this moment, which passed as swiftly as a blink of an eye, that he was lifted out of the battle. He remembered the words Mirabai had taught him,

> "Be awake to the Name!
> To be born in a human body is rare,
> Don't throw away the reward of your past good deeds.
> Life passes in an instant— the leaf doesn't go back to the branch.
> The ocean of rebirth sweeps up all beings hard,

Pulls them into its cold-running, fierce, implacable currents.
Giridhara, your name is the raft, the one safe-passage over.
Take me quickly.
All the awake ones travel with Mira, singing the name.
She says with them: Get up, stop sleeping—
the days of a life are short."

A great swirl lifted Altair up as he raised his sword, and then something pulled him up above all of this, and then a more powerful surge, like a power tearing him away from the battlefield, the carnage, the sadness and the loss. Then Altair saw in the air beside him the Sanyasi standing calmly looking at him.

"You will meet your three wives again. They are very dear to you and will be always. You will know them by this. One will be a dancer, one a singer and one an actress. Though you will try to hold on to them you cannot. You can only ever free them by letting them go. You can try anything you wish, marriage, children, but the law of karma is very clear. Trust in the flow of life. Go well Altair. Go well my child."

Then she was gone into the storm.

CHAPTER 7

On the Road to Sarnath

"Have you travelled the road to Sarnath?"

"Once only," said Henry after lunch one day. "I took a cab, but you can walk it. It's about ten kilometers."

"That's where the Buddha taught the Dharma after being enlightened isn't it?"

"Yes, Buddha traveled to Sarnath himself to teach and establish the Sangha, as he had seen that the five enlightened ones he was supposed to form the community with would be there."

"So it's not too far."

"Not at all. If you leave early in the morning, at sunrise, you can spend all day there and be back by nightfall."

"I know I have to go tomorrow. I don't know why, I just have to go. There is something important that will happen if I do."

"Ah, many mysterious things happen on the road to Sarnath," said Henry with a twinkle in his eye.

Altair started his journey on the road to Sarnath with a feeling of jubilant exhilaration. Something in the hidden wisdom of Sarnath was about to speak to him and break free.

Babaji had said it "You will write about the unity between the Christ, Krishna and the Buddha. That inspired sons and daughters of God speak with the same truth."

Just how true this was, was about to strike a light in his heart.

The houses and markets on the roadway were filled with people looking to buy and sell and talk and listen even at this early hour when it was not too dusty and there was not so much traffic. There were the usual peddlers and beggars and cycle rickshaws trying to get him to ride with them, but Altair brushed past them all as if they were cobwebs.

He stopped to buy a mango lassi and talked to some of the locals about Sarnath. After he had been walking for about half an hour Altair found himself moving smoothly along one of the streets flanked by two men. He had no idea where they had come from or why they were there, but he felt perfectly safe as if he was with his family. His vision began to blur and the crowds around them seemed to dissipate like a mirage fading. The sky overhead was clear blue, but the air seemed to tremble.

"Where are you going?" said Altair to break the ice. One man was wearing an ochre robe and had deep-set blue eyes and curly black hair. He seemed to emit a golden hue. The other man was silent but gave off the same glimmering golden aura. Both men moved with dignity and grace and treated him with love and respect.

"To Sarnath. To meet the five who left me earlier," said the blue-eyed man.

"How did you get here?" asked Altair, puzzled as to how the men had snuck up on him unawares.

"We crossed the Ganges in one step, and entered Benares early this morning, made our alms round, bathed, ate our meal and left by the east gate of the city in time to meet you, walking towards Rishipatana Mrigadava, the rishi's deer park, like all Buddhas."

"Like all Buddhas ..." Altair's voice trailed away in stunned realization. Right ahead of them was a herd of deer grazing. He felt he must be dreaming. He was with the Buddha!

"Is this Sarnath already?"

"It is, but not as you know it," said the Buddha.

"Are they monks?" asked Altair pointing at the gathering crowds. There seemed to be thousands of people massing on what were now surrounding villages and farms.

"They will be," said the other man. "Monks and nuns, dakinis and bodhisattvas, Altair, just like me. Manjushri."

Then five men approached them.

"Here he comes, that lazy good-for-nothing Siddhartha. Such a quitter! Why would we want anything to do with him?" They spoke directly to Siddhartha and seemed not to see Altair or Manjushri. "Just ignore him, he'll soon get the message."

The Buddha took a step forward to meet the men and something changed. They all seemed to become more erect, more noble and alert, as if he deserved their respect.

They made a place for him on the grass, smoothing some patches, took his robe, brought him water and knelt at his feet.

"Welcome Siddhartha to Rishipatana Mrigadava, the Rishi's deer park. We are honored that you returned to join us here."

"I thank you for your welcome my five monks, but I am no longer Siddhartha. That is no longer my name."

"What Name should we call you by?"

"The whole world is asleep in ignorance and when we discover the truth we are no longer asleep. We are awake. Awakened Ones are called Buddha."

Slowly the scene faded as Altair gazed upon the Buddha, standing in front of him, with great love and respect.

"O Buddha, teach us what you have learned so that we too may awaken."

"What do you want to do with your life?" asked the Buddha.

"Free all beings from pain and suffering," said Altair.

The Buddha looked at Altair calmly. "Then your wish will be fulfilled."

The earth trembled, and light radiated from the Buddha's body illuminating the three thousand worlds as they were made visible to Altair.

He put out his hand and placed it gently on Altair's chest, just above the heart.

Altair's body became immovable, as if was rooted to the road to Sarnath. He suddenly felt more alive than he ever had before.

And he drew no breath at all.

He felt the people moving past him on the street, saw the hand that was placed on his heart extend out to touch the hearts of five more hearts and then they reached out to touch five more. The blood that flowed through those hearts was like an inward flow of nectar, a never-ending stream.

Suddenly Altair's breath returned. The Buddha and Manjushri were standing motionless in front of him. Altair reached out his hands and placed them in theirs.

"I am from Vimala," said Manjushri, "and I can also grant you a wish."

"I want to learn how to be the embodiment of prajna or transcendent wisdom."

"Then I can grant you universal sight, and the first sign will be when you are given a real Chintamani Stone, a Pearl of Light, manifested from the Heart of Guan Yin. You have been an acolyte of the Bodhisattva Avalokiteshvara Guan Yin, which is why you are attracted to the teachings of the Dalai Lama, whom you died defending in 1959. The second sign will be when you have a direct experience of the Pure Light of Being through the Kalachakra Tantra with the Dalai Lama. The third sign will be when you manifest the Rainbow Body, a body of pure light."

"Like Long Nu."

"Yes, you were a *naga* too, a dragon's daughter, just like her. When it is time, you will also offer the pearl back to the Buddha, which will symbolize surrendering your life and ego to All, and He will accept it."

The Buddha looked at Altair directly.

"Here at Sarnath I turned twelve wheels of Dharma ...

Keep in mind this most beautiful wood,
named by the great rishi,
where ninety-one thousand kotis of Buddhas
formerly turned the Wheel.
This place is matchless, perfectly calm,
contemplating, always frequented by deer.
In this most beautiful of parks,
whose name was given by the rishi,
I will turn the holy Wheel.

Where two or three are gathered in My Name, there
I AM"

Altair travelled south towards Bihar before he stopped at Yogananda's foundational ashram and school for Kriya Yoga. While he was waiting, he heard two monks arguing. They were having a disagreement about administrative matters and how many foreigners they should allow to stay at the ashram. Altair suddenly felt very lonely. It was near Christmas and he missed his mother Mary. He walked down the dusty street towards a hotel one of the nuns had recommended.

"$1 for your shoes," said a voice.

He turned to see an old man, a beggar, holding out an Indian 1 rupee note.

"No thank you," said Altair.

"I can take you to see Sadhu."

Altair had heard some of the miraculous stories of these holy men. He nodded.

The old man held out dirty fingers expecting something in return.

Altair dug into his pocket and pulled out a wrinkled fifty rupee note.

The old man grinned a toothless grin before gesturing for Altair to follow him down a narrow side road.

Altair walked a long way through the countryside. His pack was not that heavy, but he wished he had dropped it off at the hotel first and he hadn't made a booking yet. The sun was still some way off from setting, but Altair was calculating how long it would take him to get back when they turned a tight curve in the road and arrived at a grassy knoll with a large round rock at its base. In front of it was an old man painted in grey and yellow with a large red bindu on his forehead and a white loincloth. Other than that, he seemed to have no possessions.

The toothless man left them at that point. Altair had no idea how he was going to return or whether they had some agreement once they had finished, so he sat down at the Sadhu's feet and bowed.

"What do you want to see? You ask, and I will do it. I can lift this rock with my mind."

The Sadhu closed his eyes momentarily and to Altair's utter amazement the rock in front of them which was the size of a small man shifted upwards from the earth a few degrees.

Altair opened his mouth to speak and then closed it again.

The Sadhu opened his eyes when there was no sound in response and he gazed directly at Altair.

"What do you want?"

Altair still didn't speak.

"Ah, you are a seer."

"I am walking the path of magic and the stars," said Altair.

"Yes, a seer," said the Sadhu. "What do you seek?"

"To help free those that are bound, to help those that are suffering to find peace."

"Ah, then you are a Buddha too," said the Sadhu. "And you love Krishna."

"What do you want?" said Altair.

"Nothing I don't already have," said the Sadhu waving his hand around at the hills and countryside surrounding them. "What can you tell me?"

Something moved inside Altair like a compass finding its home. His mind began to settle. His body became the Sadhu's body and the 7 interior stars or chakras lit up like flowers in flames and then danced like planets orbiting a central sun, the heart. Altair watched the inner universe unfold, his breathing reaching a calm rhythm, content to know the universal dance would reveal something soon. Then he saw it, like a twinkle in his mind's eye.

"You are a fierce man, dynamic, thirsty for life's experiences, I see you yoking horses, strong beautiful horses. You are very headstrong. You are quite playful and childlike and honor Shiva daily. You are deeply connected to Surya the Sun. You used to be a divine mystical doctor before you became a sadhu. You have the power and shakti to quickly heal. You are a physician of the gods. You bring youth to the old and life to the dead. You raised the rock by harnessing the forces of prana, the life force. You are here alone because you are stubborn and also because you had a disappointment in life earlier on in marriage. However, you have been able to let all that go now. So there is content.

And …" Altair paused.

"What?"

"There is a ghost." Altair hesitated.

"There are many ghosts in these parts."

The hesitancy dissipated with the sun. The sun was so low Altair realized it would soon be dark. He did not want to walk back alone.

"I have to go."

As if by magic, his toothless guide reappeared grinning widely and holding out an empty palm. Altair reached into his pocket and pulled out another fifty rupee note. He turned to the Sadhu.

"Thank you."

"It is I who must thank you. What you told me …"

"I do have one question for you. How did you move the rock?"
"The same way you move the stars," said the Sadhu. "Practice."

Altair was sitting out on the balcony of what was called 'The Royal Terrace' in the City of the Octagon in the far south of the Land of the Long White Cloud, his homeland. He had finished his tour of Asia and Oceania and seen and worked at some of the best schools that area of the world had to offer, from Krishnamurti to Gandhi, Yogananda to Rabindranath Tagore, Tibetan Buddhist to Siddha Yoga, Sri Aurobindo to Steiner and Montessori. He had decided as a result of his tour to train in the teaching of performing arts for children. He kept watching the sky and imagined distant stars whirling overhead in slow motion, his eyes tearing up with the patterns of light unfolding in his vision. John, a devotee of Ramana Maharshi was encouraging Altair to devote his life to Self-Realization which he maintained was the best way to serve the world. Altair had a busy day lined up tomorrow, with two televised performances of 'Aladdin' as Aladdin, and then a televised performance for Dance Arts so he wanted to get to bed early, soon after dinner. Mana was cooking, and she was singing, a habit most of Altair's flatmates took to often. Rachel and Monica were musicians too, so it was a very laid-back musical type of gathering they always had together. It was not uncommon for Monica to sing all the way through dinner, chomping on her organic veggies in between singing about lost love or how nature was suffering under men's hands. However, as he headed back down the hallway to his bedroom there was no one else there apart from Mana.

"Hi Mana?" said Altair. "How's Tara?"

"Good," said Mana, not raising her head up from the broccoli and mushroom dish that she was stirring as it steamed vigorously. "We're going out to a movie tonight, so I won't be around for long."

"No worries," said Altair. "I'll clean up ..."

He turned into the hallway to see a bearded man dressed in black, wearing a tall black hat, a black cloak and a military uniform staring at him.

"Hey!" said Altair in shock. "What are you doing?"

The man, who was well over six feet tall ran straight towards Altair's room and through the door.

That's funny, thought Altair trying to gather his thoughts, I'm sure I locked that door this morning.

"Hey Mana, call the police!" Altair shouted. "We've got an intruder!"

Altair ran to his room, which was locked, and when he opened it he looked around and saw only the barred windows which would stop anyone from jumping through and onto the concrete two stories below. He ran out again and called back to Mana on a hunch.

"Mana call the landlord instead!"

Mana was staring at him wide-eyed as he entered the kitchen and handed him the phone.

"Yes?" A deep male voice sounded on the other end.

"Hello, it's Altair here from across the road in the Royal Terraces. Look, something strange happened today, I've just got home and as I was making my way down the hall to my bedroom I saw a tall man …"

"About six feet tall or so dressed all in black?"

"Six feet? Dressed in black?" Altair couldn't believe what he was hearing.

"You should come right over. I've got something to show you."

Altair hurried over after telling Mana he might be late for dinner.

"Have a seat," said the landlord once Altair had come in and followed him to the lounge. "Have a look at this."

The landlord flipped open an old photo album until he came to a well-worn page and pointed to a black and white photo.

"Is this the man?"

And there he was, the tall bearded man in the black hat, dark eyes staring straight back at Altair.

Altair was stunned. "But ... how?"

"You are the third person in one hundred years to have seen him. Same fellow, tall, bearded, black hat, dressed in a military uniform with a cloak. He fought in a war all those years ago when medical technology was a lot rougher than it is now. They had to bring him back here, on a ship, after he was shot in the leg. They tried to amputate but he lost too much blood. In your very room. In those days it used to be a hospital and your room was a surgical operating room. So, sadly he didn't survive. And must be very pissed about it because he is still hanging around all these years later. Not sure what you can do. Say a prayer. Maybe."

So, Altair did. And the ghost never bothered him again. Altair dealt with the ghost in the same way Jesus had taught him to deal with demons. Very clear confident intention and surrender to the power of love and God to intervene and do whatever was necessary to free and liberate this soul.

"By the power of Christ begone." Three times.

And so, it was. Because with the power of love and faith anything can be accomplished. Altair was witnessing the power of love and faith in the flow of life manifesting all around him.

"Truly I tell you, if you have faith as small as a mustard seed, you can say to this mountain, 'Move from here to there,' and it will move. Nothing will be impossible for you."

This little passage from Matthew was such a treasure of wisdom that Altair could scarcely believe it was not being taught at the highest levels of all business and education. He could see how anything he truly believed and wished with deep pure intention was coming true.

His path of magic and the stars was even revealing itself through his friends. One night he was talking about love and friendship with his best friend BB and suddenly he disappeared into a star that appeared in her eye and she disappeared into his. They were both shocked and wondered how many other portals like this would appear when love was present.

Dreams and visions were not something out there and untouchable but were an intrinsic part of the fabric of reality. Along with imagination, dreams and visions were yogic siddhis or powers that with practice through meditation could become the foundations of our actions and signs along our path.

CHAPTER 8

Pleiades

Altair climbed the grey stairs to his family home and pushed the double white doors into all the noise. They opened onto the dining room and lounge. The air was hot and filled with the noise of celebrations, welcoming him home from the Deep South. The room had a big oval oak table around which a number of his friends were sitting. On the right was the family library piled with books and on the left were all the family photo albums and pictures his mother Mary loved to display. Something made his skin get goosebumps and his heart race. He knew his best friend Faith loved to matchmake and she had warned him she might bring someone special. Faith was also from the Deep South, a pixie creature who loved to sniff lavender with Altair and his other best friend Sid the Tibetan Monk and together they would all go crazy in the shopping centers having races with the supermarket trolleys. As he stood there, knowing the magic Faith could bring to any occasion, his eyes turned to the far corner of the room by the wedding photograph of his parents and he saw her. Their eyes met and they both smiled, and he was smitten instantly. She was watching him and returned to playing a harmonica. He walked over to her amidst the smiles and choruses of 'Welcome Home'.

"Hello," he said. "I'm Altair."

"I know," she said. "I'm Priya."

"Do you play the harmonica?"

"No, just learning." And she smiled at Faith like they knew a secret.

"Oh? You're pretty good! You're not a musician then?"

"No, I love to dance," said Priya.

And that was it. Like two peas in a pod Altair and Priya sat and talked the whole evening as if no one else in the entire world existed and he knew that this was the sign he'd been looking for. The Dancer the Sanyasi had told him about, his first wife from his life as a Raj. He knew it with all his heart and all his soul. And just now they had found a way into each other's world.

Priya was small and slight, almost elfin, with the determination of a tiger and the mystique of the Sphinx. She had a keen sharp intelligence like a knife and could cut away Altair's concerns like butter. Her eyes were hazel and her hair curly and tawny brown and she smelled like sweet honey. Love, especially deep true love, has a way of working magic with the stars.

And so, it did.

"Priya," said Altair one day, many moons into their relationship, after a dream where they both dreamed of flying the same crystal airplane. Altair dreamt he was flying Priya and she was in the back. Priya dreamed Altair was flying her and he was in the front. "Tell me about where you want to fly to. Where is your bridge across forever? What other worlds does it lead to?"

Priya looked deep into Altair's eyes. "I want to explore the stars with you. That's why we fell in love. You can help me go beyond what is here. To find out what lies beyond."

"What did that Steve guy say about other worlds?"

Priya and Altair had just attended a seminar on extraterrestrials and other worlds with Steve, a US expert on extraterrestrial contact and had decided to sign up together for a weekend workshop with him. It had been Faith, their divine connector and fountain of everything spiritual who had told them about it. Faith seemed to have her pulse on every esoteric heartbeat in town and could weave magical relationships where before there were none. Priya adored her like a goddess.

"He said something about this Venus and Jupiter energy in the spine. That we were like universal connectors or cosmic radio stations for the universe and life out there."

"I want to find out how it works."

"Why do you want to find out about life out there so much? What about life here? I mean I want to know but there is so much everyone needs here on earth."

"I know, I can't explain all of it, but I've wanted to explore the stars and other worlds since I was a child."

"You've got an alien inside you," laughed Priya. "That should be enough."

"Well, I figure we are all like that. We just don't know it. We all come from the stars."

"That guy Steve is just like you, Altair. Weird. When you look into his eyes he looks like he comes from another planet."

"I thought so too. He seems like he has some answers to all this."

Steve certainly did have answers. He had been a professional rugby league international totally disinterested in UFOs and that sort of thing, when one weekend, when he was on holiday at Babylon Beach, he had been struck down by a blue light which came from the stars and the beings he connected with downloaded him with information from an extraterrestrial civilization that was in direct contact with earth. It had changed his life overnight. And it was about to change Altair and Priya's.

The workshop was a massive energy shift. Altair and Priya felt like they were surfing a wave. It started with all the participants, which included Faith and her friend Hina, cleansing the chakras by replacing the crystals that composed the petals of those chakras. They worked on the third eye or Ajna chakra, which had two petals, for most of the time. Then they worked on telepathy with partners. Altair's partner was Hina and using simple energy breathing techniques in the spine they were able to reach out and touch each other's essence. When Altair tried it with Hina he got an enormous shock. As he entered her consciousness Hina shape-shifted and formed a ferocious tiger which sprang out at him, claws and all. It was a stunning, confronting demonstration of power in its rawest form. Hina confirmed that was exactly what she had manifested, and she seemed impressed that Altair had picked up so exactly on it.

"I'm not comfortable with men," she said quite candidly. "You're the first man I've allowed to get anywhere near me on that psychic level. My mum has always protected me from unwanted forces. She taught me how to deal with it. Like this."

"I want to find a way through," said Altair. "A bridge. Into your world. Into your being."

"I'm not ready for that," said Hina. "I prefer to live within my walls. I know I'm safe that way."

"Powerful walls!" said Altair.

That night both Altair and Priya were exhausted but they couldn't sleep.

"What did you discover?" said Altair.

"Amazing energies," said Priya. "All over my body. Like a zinging up and down my spine. As if everything electrical in my body has been suddenly activated."

"Me too," said Altair.

They lay awake a long time thinking of the stars and the magic that lay beyond them on the bridge across forever.

Steve was a hard taskmaster. Priya and Altair signed up for a number of weekend workshops after that initial one. One Saturday night Steve said in front of the group,

"I'd like to give you all feedback about your progress. Tough stuff to help you."

He went around the group praising some and advising others how to fine tune their energies.

To Priya he said, "You have a pristine energy, very pure and awake, like a new birth."

Priya smiled her delicious warm smile that Altair loved so much.

Finally, he turned to Altair.

"You," he said, "pretend to be the most spiritual of all, but you have the most to learn because you are the least spiritually developed."

Altair sat a long while after the circle sharing, in shock and silence.

When they got home he asked Priya, "Do you really think I am that immature?"

She laughed. "You take yourself too seriously. Steve said that to wake you up."

Altair worried about the after-effects of this all weekend. He mulled and stewed over it all week.

The next weekend was the last workshop where they would all go to Babylon Beach to call craft in from the stars. There was a part of Altair, a sulking part, that didn't believe this would happen to him right now. Maybe for the others but not to him.

They all sat high on a hillside above the beach as a group and called the craft in using the Venus Jupiter techniques in the spine that Steve had taught them. Blue lights appeared in the sky and on the horizon and flew at them from all angles.

It was Contact, but not as Altair wanted it.

Perhaps it was something in the look he had that night, perhaps it was a hunch, or perhaps it was what Steve had said to Altair that shifted things so much because as time passed Altair began to question whether he would ever have true Contact. He had seen, and he believed but he hadn't felt. He couldn't put his finger on exactly what he wanted from the stars and magic, but he knew he wanted more.

He was appointed Director of an educational institution in the Deep South and Priya and he started a family together. There were no more joyful moments than the birth of a son and then a daughter, both of them treasures in his heart that he knew would be there always.

"I'm never apart from you," he would whisper to them when they were alone. "I'm a part of you and you're a part of me. We're part of each other. Every day of my life you will be in my heart and even beyond this life too."

Altair wrote birth songs for both of his children. They lived all together beside a beautiful beach. He travelled the world marketing for education. Priya and Altair went through the joys and struggles of all couples. And still, he wondered.

One day Steve returned to the Deep South, invited by Altair to give a seminar on extraterrestrial contact.

That evening, on a Saturday, after the talk, Altair and Steve were sitting eating pizza together. Priya was at home with the children.

"What did you think of the seminar?" asked Steve sipping a beer.

"People get very excited by extraterrestrials. Why don't they reveal themselves?"

"It's a simple matter of energy and consciousness. You've seen it for yourself. When you raise the energy levels in your system you attract wherever your attention is focused. Like a radio beacon, you tune into the right frequency. You tune into them with the right energy and they will tune into you. And find you."

Steve paused.

"Do you want to see a starcraft?"

Altair couldn't believe his ears.

"Right here? Now?"

They were eating at a beachfront restaurant near his house.

"Sure, right here. Let's go for a walk."

They took a stroll along the beach past a number of people who were also out late. It was just going on 1 am. There was a woman with a dog, a man out fishing in a boat, a couple walking on the beach. Most people's lights were out. It was a beautiful evening and the sky was very clear and littered with stars.

"Let's stop here," said Steve.

They stopped not far from Altair's beachfront house.

"You remember the Venus Jupiter exercises?"

"Sure."

"So simply visualize building the energy within the spine as you connect to the emerald green of Venus on the left. Then connect to the craft through the ruby red energy of Jupiter on the right and extend the energy out through the third eye to make contact."

Altair and Steve did the exercises together for about five minutes. They were both adept at it and the consciousness flowed easily and smoothly. They gazed up at the heavens together.

A few minutes passed, and a satellite appeared around about the center of the Pleiades constellation and started to move across the sky as they watched.

It reached the center of the sky and stopped.

Stopped.

"It ... it stopped!" said Altair, scarcely believing his eyes. "Satellites don't stop!"

"Right," said Steve.

As Altair watched in disbelief the satellite began to lower, vertically, from its position high up in the stars, and descend towards them. As it grew closer and larger, Altair began to make out details.

A starcraft was right above them, transparent so they could see the stars through it, with three lights at the nose and the two wing tips, and an enormous booster engine at the rear. It was gigantic, about the size of two jumbo jets and it descended over Altair's house. All activity on the beach had stopped and those witnessing just stood there stunned. The craft manoeuvred over Altair's house before flashing three times in a sign to Altair and then a whooshing sound could be heard as the craft sped off and disappeared at a rate faster than anything Altair has seen move to this day. He stood there, rooted to the spot.

"Did ..." was all he could say.

"Yes," said Steve. "Now go home to Priya. She will be missing you. Watch what happens carefully these next few days. And do not report what happened or how you called the craft to the authorities. They will be all over you and you will be tracked forever. Just like the X-Files. Keep the information safely among your friends."

Altair nodded. He was still rocked by the energies, by the possibilities for humanity, by the knowledge that we could make Contact if we wished, if we raised our energies, if we knew how.

And he knew how.

The following days were filled with the news of the 'alien contact'. In newspapers and television, stories of the craft from eyewitnesses appeared and the United States Air Force flew two jets in to the beach resort with scientists in white coats who posted rewards around the town of $500 for information leading to or pertaining to the extraterrestrial craft. Four young boys who had been sleeping out on the roof of their house had been 'visited' by the starship and described exactly the same craft as Altair had seen, the whooshing noise and the incredible speed with which it left their location after it hovered above them. Friends and family who knew of Altair's experience all wanted to know more. And everyone who laid claim to an alien contact or alien DNA came out of the woodwork.

Two weeks later Altair was walking along another beach on the same coast a little further north with five of his friends. They were joking with him about his Contact.

"So, you can cross worlds," said Rihanna.

"And call extraterrestrial craft," said Brynn.

"Go on, show us," they all cajoled him.

"You can do it," whispered Rihanna. "Go on, I know you can do anything."

Rihanna had been good friends with Altair for such a long time. She was convinced that she walked the same path and they often shared their mystical experiences.

"Now?" said Altair. "In the middle of the day? The craft came at 1 am. From the stars. The Pleiades. If I call it now you might never see it. What would be just as good a test?"

"The dolphins," said Rihanna. "Call the dolphins."

"The dolphins," they all cried. There was lots of laughter and a good feeling about this suggestion. If anyone could do it Altair could.

"How do you do it?" said Brynn. "Is there an actual bridge or what?"

"Just an intention," said Altair. "Then an activation of the current in your body through the Venus and Jupiter exercises. They are very similar to Yogananda's Kriya Yoga. Then surrender. And wait. That's it basically. A call of the heart. If my heart is in tune with theirs they will come."

"Show me," said Rihanna.

"All right," said Altair. "I'll show you." And he sat down on the beach and closed his eyes.

For a moment all he heard was the tumble and falling of the waves, swish, swish. Everything else was quiet.

He focused on the dolphins, bringing them to his mind's eye. Then he made an intention to become the ocean and began to breathe and draw the Venus and Jupiter energies up through the left and right sides of his body. It only took a few minutes. Then something happened.

As he relaxed his mind into the shape of the ocean waves a new consciousness began to sweep around his body and powers he had hitherto been unexposed to rose to the surface. He felt for all the world like a dolphin, leaping and diving in and out of the ocean sprays. He felt safe and filled with joy under the water. He could breathe!

"Look, look!" came the cry. Altair opened his eyes.

The five friends were pointing out to sea. There, swimming along the beach, was a pod of dolphins. Three of them turned and swam into the beach at just the point Altair was sitting.

Altair rose to his feet, feeling at one with the dolphins. He could hear them, feel them calling to him.

"C'mon!" he shouted.

But his friends were too shocked by the sudden appearance of the dolphins to move. They stood there with open mouths, gaping as Altair took off his clothes and dived into the surf. The dolphins waited, playing close to the shore and when Altair joined them they swam with him out to sea, circling and frolicking, jumping and greeting him with clicks and whistles. Altair could understand all that passed between them that day. He could see the worlds they came from, the joy they brought to this world, the sadness they felt at the atrocities committed to their brethren and the damage done to the ocean. They were such peace-loving light-filled beings. He felt more at home with them here than he did in many other places on this planet. He knew they were his dolphin light family come to acknowledge him.

Where Priya was smart and elfin, Rihanna was passionate and mysterious. She had large dark eyes and black curly hair and she and Altair had an uncanny connection. His meeting with his star family, which is how he referred to the extraterrestrials and his light family, the dolphins, had opened a way from this world into others. Telepathy with Rihanna became as easy and natural as breathing, even without trying. Altair would suddenly find himself in her dreams, so he would call her, and she would confirm, "Yes, I was wearing a white dress with a necklace of pearls." They could be in separate rooms and shown an object or given something to touch and they would both have an identical experience. Rihanna could hold a pack of cards, secretly draw a sequence and Altair could tell her what they were.

They had discovered this by accident one night when they were all in a meditation group. It was shortly after a trip to India and the Himalayas that Altair had made to see Swami Shyam. When Altair came back he was literally glowing. Everyone noticed it. Altair discovered on his return that by raising the energies up his spine while holding an intention he could trigger a similar energy in anyone that looked into his eyes. He knew this was the *Naga* energies working through him. One night as they were going around the circle and people were asking Altair to activate this energy or that intention, when he reached Rihanna he suddenly felt himself raised up and leaving his body and an instant later found himself in her body. It was most uncanny and incredibly unnerving and greatly upset Priya and Rihanna's husband Brynn. They wanted Altair and Rihanna to stop immediately which they did but the natural consequence of this unexpected skill was the desire to experiment. So consciously and unconsciously in dreams, the telepathy between the two of them unfolded and it led to a great rift between Altair and Priya.

One night Altair was talking to Priya while she was taking a bath. The children were fast asleep. He looked into her eyes and he knew something was amiss. They had been too close and the love that sparkles can also burn.

"Are you having a relationship with her?"

Altair paused a long time.

"Are you having a relationship with her?"

"No," said Altair, "you know we're not," but he knew it was too late. Nothing he could say would make any difference. She had already left him in her heart and that was what mattered.

Tears filled Altair's eyes and then Priya knew that he knew too.

"I want out," she said simply with typical elfin defiance.

Altair's spirit was crushed in that instant and his heart broke in two. An anger, a fierce burning smouldering centuries-old anger emerged from the ashes of his broken heart.

"Aaargh!" he shouted as his anger boiled over and he slammed his fist into the wall.

Priya was horrified.

"No," she said as she rose out of the bath. "No!"

Altair had no intention of hurting anyone, but he recognized the past life of a soldier where he had faced off enemies over love before.

Altair stormed out of the house, ran down the road and emitted the most horrendous flood of expletives over the phone to his poor mother. When he had calmed down he wept uncontrollably. His mother was silent a long while.

"Why don't you come home for a while."

Altair thought about this for a long time.

"No, I need to sort this out with her. For the children's sake."

Altair was trembling badly when he returned. His nervous system had taken such a shock. It might have been the delayed reaction to Priya's ultimatum or it might have been finding himself in a totally new reality from the one he had thought he was in just an hour or two ago. He knew this was part of his journey across the bridge between worlds because wherever there was light there was also darkness. And both had to be understood in the path of love and wisdom. Knowing that did not make things any easier, however.

"I need out. I want to have the freedom to explore," said Priya a few days later.

Altair felt helpless. His childhood, so filled with hope and trust and beautiful nurturing was now crashing down all around him and he was alone.

"I'll move out," said Altair.

"I'm not asking you to do that," said Priya. "The children want to see you."

"I'll move into the cave."

"Up to you."

The cave was the garden shed. In order to be near to the children, Altair decided on an impulse to convert the shed in their backyard, which usually held gardening tools and which he had nicknamed the cave as it was so dark, into a meditation cave. He pulled out the tools and hung Thangka of the Buddha and the scroll of Saraswati and made an altar with the Masters of Krishna and Babaji's line. And he always carried a little statue of Mary and baby Jesus which reminded him that no matter how much suffering he was going through, someone was going through more.

Rihanna helped him a great deal in that terrible time. They both decided to drop all connections of a mystical and telepathic nature which included meditation group gatherings to give Altair a chance to heal.

"So, what do you want to do?" asked Rihanna one Sunday afternoon.

"I feel so broken," said Altair. "I need to heal. The only thing I can think of is helping others."

"I'm the manager for all the intellectually disabled groups here in the Deep South," said Rihanna. "If there is anything you can think of that could help them, then I can arrange it."

"You know me well," said Altair managing a small smile. "If there is any way you could use my yoga and meditation experience or performing arts ..."

"Didn't you do an OT job once?" said Rihanna.

It was true. Some years before, Altair had dated a doctor, Estella. She was in charge of a large hospital wing and their OT, the occupational therapist, had a sudden family emergency and took three months off. As Altair was there and he had a counselling degree they employed him to fill in, doing everything from art to yoga to tai chi and meditation. Altair had lots of close run-ins with patients as he worked in the psychiatric ward. One day a patient named Bill knocked the orderly clean out. He then stalked other doctors and nurses who were all too afraid of him to go near. Altair had just arrived, didn't know this had all just happened and came around the corner to be picked up by Bill, who was a mammoth of a man.

"I'm gonna kill ya!" said Bill.

Altair wasn't frightened, but he also couldn't breathe, caught in a behemoth's bear hug.

"Scared?"

Because he couldn't speak or resist and was feeling like his ribs were going to crack the only thing Altair could do was relax. He let all the life go out of his body and hung limp.

Suddenly Bill dropped him.

"Fooled ya!"

He picked Altair up from a heap on the floor.

"I wouldn't 'ave killed ya. I like ya."

And Bill turned around and walked away into the arms of the security guards who had arrived.

Altair's memories returned to Rihanna.

"I guess I could do that," he said. "Set me up with a date and I'll see what I can come up with."

He relied on his OT experience and built a program with Rihanna where he taught the residents of the houses under her direction everything from yoga to tai chi, massage to meditation, art, and music. It was just as much therapy for him as for the residents.

Altair remembered a profound moment in those six months where something began to switch back on for him.

He was doing a meditation exercise with one of the groups and all was very silent. There was a deep still presence and everything was in harmony. Suddenly Colin, one of the residents opened his eyes wide in awareness and alarm.

"Here!" he said, pointing to his head again and again. "Listen! I can hear my brain clicking!"

The cave was a difficult place. Every night after Altair went home he would play with the children, kiss them good night and head out to the cave. If Priya went out he would stay in the house, only to disappear into the cave when he heard her car pull into the garage.

"What's it like," asked Rihanna one day at one of the resident's houses, "living in a cave?"

"For the first few months it was terrible," confessed Altair. "I had this image from a wee boy of Horton the elephant sitting on Maisie's egg, and I figured if I could sit long enough with the pain, that one day it would hatch into something different, like a rebirth. Nice idea, but life isn't always like that.

In those months I would go into the cave, and I'd try to sit, and I'd sit, in desperate hope like Horton, but most of the time my heart would hammer, and I couldn't breathe, and I'd have to get up and walk around in the garden and look at the stars until the feelings subsided. It was such a dark time!"

"You should have told me. You could have gone out or done something with Brynn and me."

"I was too low, too ashamed to show my head in public. I felt people were silently laughing at me and my situation. I'd lost my marriage, my kids, my job ..."

Altair hung his head.

"Your job? I didn't know that."

"Yep. The Board of Directors decided I was too vulnerable down here, so they transferred me up North. Brought a new director in. Didn't give me an option of staying. So, I resigned."

"What will you do?"

"I'm thinking of starting another company with some friends. When I heal. Not until then."

Altair had been putting on a brave face by not letting Rihanna see just how low he'd been, how much fear he'd had to face. He'd always talked about mastering fear and being in love, and here he was unable to simply be and forgive and nurture himself.

He decided to let his guard down a little more.

"Sometimes I have the craziest thoughts," he told her. "I just want to go and smash things. Like the Hulk. I guess it's a habit I have from those 16th century Raj days." He let out a small smile. "It kind of feels good to have those thoughts, to know I'm not going to act on them, but to let out a little wickedness, a little of my wild side."

"How do you deal with it?" asked Rihanna. "All those pent-up feelings. It can't be good for you to lock them all away."

"You're right," said Altair. "The main thing is not to do harm to any other human being, no matter how strongly you feel or how angry you are at them. When I feel like that I take myself away, high up into the mountains and forests for a day or two. Into the wilderness by myself. The first time I did it I felt such madness overtake me that I found a huge log and pounded enormous rocks for hours until I was exhausted. Then I cried and cried for just as long a time until I was all spent. It was perhaps the most healing thing I have done for myself. Self-compassion. Taking the time to be alone and get in touch with where my heart was truly at. To be totally present with those feelings, no matter how awful I thought they were. That is the only way to move beyond them."

Tears filled Altair's eyes.

"And slowly they changed, and I made friends with them, this terrible rage, this crippling anger, this enormous pain that I had carried around like a weight."

He took a deep breath.

"They were my own personal demons, they were the parts of me I feared the most."

Rihanna gave him a hug.

"It's much better when you share."

"You're right, that's exactly what my Mum says."

And both of their eyes filled with tears at the same time.

CHAPTER 9

Potalaka

Altair was alone in the cave. After six months he began to look more deeply into his journey across the bridge between worlds as his mind and heart grew calmer. He saw more of the light, because he now saw more of the darkness.

He began to question the nature of consciousness itself. If everything around him and within him was God or Source or Buddha, then surely he could communicate with that pure consciousness like he did with extraterrestrials, dolphins and Rihanna.

He let his mind grow calm and surrendered to the stillness within the cave.

At first, nothing happened. Altair knew not to expect anything. He just sat still with his inner eye fixed on the third eye area and waited. He noticed the silence. He sent out a soul call to the One, the Source of All Love, like a dart filled with the desire to see the Beloved and he rested In total faith that an answer would come.

Altair became aware of a subtle change. The air around him became still as if matching the presence he felt within. The consciousness that was the air began to arrange itself like a living cosmos and he could feel tendrils of that consciousness reaching out to touch him, the awareness that he called Altair.

He felt the hairs prickle on the back of his neck. He became aware of the cave and the paintings and statues, the lawn outside, the garden, Priya and the children sleeping, the house and other houses with people asleep in the neighborhood, the beach that started just down at the end of the street, the waves and the great ocean that the waves were part of, the waves that were conscious, the ocean that was breathing, the sky above that was listening, the stars looking down, everything connected, to us.

It was as if he had connected to the heart of the world, the mind of the cosmos. The stars themselves were whirling and spiraling around him, jumping and diving in the universal currents.

Then he heard a voice and saw a face in front of him. It could have been Swami Shyam or Sai Baba. Mother Mary or Guan Yin.

All it said was,

"Sleep. Remember your dreams and visions, meditate upon them. Then act. Sleep, child."

So, he did.

His dream was simple and very clear. Sai Baba came to him in the dream.

"Visit Sam. Tell him I want to see him. That is all you need to do. When it is time I will come to you in another form, as a Chintamani Stone in the form of a pearl and Amrita in the form of nectar. Until then, know that the living consciousness of All That Is comes to you in the form of the Masters. All of them, Christ, Krishna, Buddha, Muhammad, Thoth, All Divine Mothers are all embodiments of the one pure existence, consciousness and bliss that is Love and Wisdom and speak the same truth with One Voice."

When he woke he took a deep breath, pushed the covers back and opened the garden shed door. The morning was bright and filled with wonder. He could feel his heart racing with fresh new blood, a cosmic detective on the trail of the greatest mystery of all. Life.

He didn't go in for breakfast, he got straight in his car and drove over to Sam's place. He had known Sam for years. Sam was a friend of both he and Priya and Rihanna's and a wild man when it came to love. He had no end of female suitors pursuing him, but he always claimed he was free and open so no one woman ever lasted long. He was still in bed when Altair called.

"Sam, wake up!"

"Altair, are you nuts? I'm not awake. Go away. Go home. Do something useful with your life!"

"I had a dream about Sai Baba. He came to me and told me he wants to see you."

There was complete silence.

"Sam?" Altair opened the door and walked in. Sam was lying awake on the sofa in the lounge.

"I had the same dream. Sai Baba told me he wants me to go and see him in India."

"Are you going?"

"Nah, I always believe in three signs. Tell me if he visits you again."

Altair walked out, irritated. Surely Sam wasn't that stupid.

He drove into town and had to get some cash out before he started work. He stopped at an ATM machine just next to the cathedral.

There was a woman standing in front of him in the line at the machine. She was taking a long time withdrawing her cash. Altair hummed a tune impatiently. He didn't want to be late for his first meeting.

The woman turned around, but instead of leaving she stared straight at, or rather through Altair.

"Tell your friend Sam he needs to come and see Sai Baba in India."

Then she turned on her heel and walked off into the early morning breakfast crowd.

Altair now knew he must find a Chintamani Stone in the form of a pearl. Both Sai Baba and Manjushri had mentioned it. But where? He knew it would come from the heart of Guan Yin but what did that mean? The only answers ever came when he surrendered totally to the stillness, and right now he had to attend a meeting. He was late when he arrived. He was dreamy when he was supposed to be concentrating on their next marketing trip to Europe.

"What?" asked Altair.

"You should go on your own," said Mick.

"You're the most experienced," said Angelique. She looked at Altair with concern.

"Are you OK? No sleep?"

"Right," said Altair.

"Get a coffee at the break. The Arts Centre has the best."

"The Arts Centre? But I don't drink coffee."

Angelique laughed. "That's code for 'take a decent break'. Walk off those blues."

Altair took the hint. As business partners, Mick and Angelique had been very good to him. Allowing him time away from the business whenever he needed it. After an hour, he walked down to the Arts Centre, which was full of crazy stalls and market bargains at any time of the year.

"Want custom clothes?" asked Colleen, the auburn-haired woman at ZigZag. She dealt in one-off clothing and Altair rather liked what she imported.

"This top is great," said Altair, choosing a pattern of black, red, green, and white that he had never seen before. "How about the bottoms?"

"Sorry," said Colleen. "Strangely a young woman bought them this morning just before you came here. Striking blonde. Said she wanted them for a singing audition. Didn't want the top."

Altair looked at Colleen for a moment. "Oh well, if they are supposed to get back together they will," he said.

Pity, he thought, they would have looked so good together.

Altair slept fitfully in the cave that night, filled with dreams of dakinis, the sky dancers that beckoned him on the one hand into the light and demons on the other that enticed him into the dark. He was drowsy when he woke and hurried into the house once he saw Priya's car drive off with the children for school. He had a band meeting after work where he was auditioning a new singer and he wanted to make sure he had all the music. He made tea and toasted barley bread with Manuka honey. As well as starting a company he also had formed a band, so his world was taking shape again.

As so often happens, things that look good together, find each other again, no matter how slim the odds.

"What song do you want to do first up?" said Paul. Paul was a doctor, guitarist and lyricist extraordinaire. Paul and Altair were rehearsing at a friend's house near the beach.

"An original," said Altair. "That will give her a better feeling for what we are about."

"Agreed."

"What's her name again?"

"Aria."

"Good name for a singer."

"I think that's her now."

A blue Toyota pulled up outside on the road between the beach and the house. They watched a blonde woman in a green tie-dye dress get out. They had advertised for a new singer so had auditioned a few before today.

"Did you check her stars?" grinned Paul.

"Not yet," smiled Altair.

"I would, you're pretty spot on with that sort of stuff."

"I used to be, I haven't touched it in a while."

The door opened and a woman with sparkling blue eyes strode in. She held out her hand to Altair.

"Hi, I'm Aria."

"Altair, and this is Paul."

"Shall I sing first?"

"Why not?"

And that was it. She set up the music stand she'd brought with her as if she were giving a concert on a stage and began to sing.

She had the voice of a nightingale and couldn't keep her eyes off Altair. There was no doubting their connection. Altair could feel it from the moment she walked in. When she had finished she was the consummate professional.

"Will you let me know?"

"Sure," said Altair. "You have a beautiful voice."

"Thank you," she said with an equally beautiful smile and she left.

Paul was silent for a few moments. He hadn't spoken at all in the time she was there.

"She had eyes for you man."

"I noticed," said Altair. "She has an amazing voice."

"There are lots of good voices."

"I felt something. Something old. Something very familiar."

Something had stirred in Altair.

"She knows what she wants man, that's all I'm saying."

Altair wasn't listening. Just like he hadn't listened to his good friends Tim and Deon or his Mum when they'd talked to him early on about Priya.

That was his hubris. A stubborn pride when it came to love. Yet uncannily and in spite of everything, Aria would accompany him to one of the greatest treasures of all, a Chintamani Stone, from the Goddess of Deep Listening Herself, Avalokiteshvara Guan Yin.

Altair and Aria quickly formed a love duet and a musical partnership. On their first date something extraordinary happened, a sign to make sure he wouldn't miss their connection.

They were back at Aria's place after a restaurant outing. Altair happened to walk past her bedroom on the way back from the bathroom and sneaked a look, as the door was open. There on the bed were a pair of pants. An unmistakable pattern of black, red, green, and white. He couldn't believe his eyes.

"Aria can I ask you something?" he said when he returned to the lounge.

"Sure," she smiled expectantly.

"I noticed a pair of pants in your bedroom, an unusual pattern. Where did you get them from?"

"Oh," she looked puzzled. "A lady at the Arts Centre. They were a pair actually, but I didn't want the top. Why?"

"You won't believe this, but I bought the top the very same day as you bought the bottoms. I must have just missed you buying them. From the lady at the Arts Centre."

So, it continued, from this unmistakable sign to another and another.

But something was missing in his heart. He had tried going through months of counselling with Priya in the hope of winning her back but all she ever said was "I don't want this relationship." That was devastating enough on top of the pain that comes along with the actual separation. The children were doing OK, but Altair was suffering. He realized just how much when Priya announced one day that she had met Brandon, an airline pilot with the same birthday as her. And that they were taking the children to Europe and wanted Altair's permission. Altair agreed with a heavy heart. He had watched his son Leo born in water under the constellation Leo and his daughter Ursa born in their living room. He wept a long time with his children on the night they left for Brandon's home in the capital of his motherland. Then Altair tried to pick up the pieces of his life.

Aria wanted to sing in Europe, so Altair decided to accompany her. He had marketing to do for the new company he had set up, so they travelled Europe together, singing in King's and Queen's ballrooms in picturesque castles nestled in the Alps, doing duets for opera companies in London and eating pizza with world-renowned musicians in the Cotswolds.

They returned to the Deep South and had to choose whether to continue on and live in Europe or move to the US.

That night Altair had a dream. He was standing on a beach in Los Angeles and three dolphins swam along and one stood on its tail and waved to him.

"We've got to go to America," said Altair and he told Aria his dream.

"Then we will," she said, and they flew out the following morning.

Three days later they were standing on the Jade Palace beach and three dolphins swam along and one stood on its tail and waved to him.

Altair and Aria stayed with relatives right on the coast. They arrived the day after a massive earthquake in which their uncle's swimming pool had slipped 1.5 meters into the neighbors' property. That day Altair drove to the local grocery store to pick up some organic veggies to cook for dinner and some grains to soak for breakfast. As he was leaving the store he noticed a young girl crying on the sidewalk.

"Is there anything I can do to help?"

"I'm homeless," she said. She looked up at him through a tear-soaked face and then began to sob again. She must have been no more than fifteen years old thought Altair.

"I'll tell you what," he said with a smile. "I've just bought these groceries for the family for tonight. There's enough to feed one person for a week. Why don't you have them?"

He knelt down in the road in front of her and placed the bags at her feet.

She looked up at him and then rubbed her eyes in bewilderment and then shock.

"What's that, what's … that … at your shoulder …"

She could hardly breathe or get her words out.

Altair felt it first and then saw it. The most serene calm came over him as if he too had gone past his last breath and was floating somewhere indescribable in human terms. He looked just past his left shoulder and saw the most magnificent glow, like a million suns, concentrated in a ball behind him. A tall beneficent female form reached out past him towards the girl's heart.

"It's an angel!" she cried.

And indeed, it was.

A gift from God sent in this most unlikely of places to bring redemption from pain and freedom from suffering.

Years later Altair would learn Her Name.

Auriel.

Something had happened, and Altair knew it. The One Consciousness we call God or Source was communicating to him through the most unlikely channels, dreams, dolphins, a homeless girl and an angel. The angel was a distinct sign and it galvanized him into action. He and Aria headed north, working for a spiritual publishing house then singing as they went to Festivals and yoga groups at beautiful lake shrines, yoga villages and spiritual communities. One night when they reached Canada they stayed with Jackie, a yoga teacher on Vancouver Island. None of them could have predicted what came next.

"Altair, how is your search for magic and the stars unfolding?" asked Jackie.

Altair laughed. "Slowly. I'm waiting for the One Consciousness to speak to me when it's ready."

"No more angels?"

"Just the ones I see around me," said Altair with a smile gesturing at the guests attending Jackie's dinner party.

"That's what I wanted to speak to you about. Do you see that couple over there?" She nodded towards the doorway. A couple looked just about ready to leave.

Altair nodded back.

"They heard you read the stars and wondered if you had time to read theirs."

"When?"

"Tonight, if possible. They're having marriage troubles. I have a small room out back you can use."

"Sure. Tell them yes. I can do the reading for them in about an hour. Can you get their details?"

An hour later Altair found himself sitting across from the couple he had just met. Jennifer and Dave were having a great deal of trouble even listening to each other when they came in. Altair settled them down with presence and meditation.

"OK, I want you to breathe with me. God is sitting here in both of you. Your breath is God's breath and your words are God's sacred words of the One Shared Heart," Altair began.

He asked them to visualize that breath of God rising and falling in a cycle around the interior planets of the chakras.

He asked them what their God-Self would each want from the relationship.

Then he began to read their soul path, both individually and together.

An hour later and they both came out of the room smiling.

They paid Altair by *Koha* which for Maori people is a gift of the heart. The Shared Heart.

The next morning a line of more than fifty people were lined up outside Jackie's door.

Jennifer and Dave had been very generous with their gratitude and sent out the word. It spread like wildfire.

All the way through Canada and the US the same lines appeared outside someone's door as if by magic, guided by the stars. When

Altair got tired he would move on to a different city, hoping to remain anonymous, but word would get around, and he would be invited to a different house and there would be a new line of people. He did it all on *Koha* and received gifts of original paintings, silver tea sets, cash and jewelry, crystals and offers of exchanges like massage, many gifts he could not carry or take up, so he gave them away. There were so many miracles that people began to call him Merlin.

A Native American Indian came to visit him. Altair had helped her with her business which had been in a slump and now two weeks after a reading with Altair and it was flourishing.

"How can I help you?"

"It's my son."

"How can I help your son?"

"It's a very difficult case."

"Nothing is too difficult for the Lord. We do nothing on our own. Everything is the will of the Lord."

"He was in an accident. He's a logger. There was an accident at the mill and he was trapped between two logs. His spine was crushed. He's in a full cast and won't get out for six months."

"How can I help?"

"Would you put something on a recording for him? There are no phones there so I need to send it by mail."

"Sure."

Then she hesitated.

"There's one more thing."

"Yes?"

"He thinks you can help him with his dream."

"What is it?"

"He wants to become an actor in Hollywood."

"Does he have a family to support?"

"Yes."

"Does he have any experience in acting?"

"No."

"And he's in a full cast with a broken back somewhere north of here with no phones."

"Right."

"I see. Give me his details and I'll see what I can do."

Altair made the recording and gave it to his mother to send to her son. He didn't hear anything for two weeks. Then one day the phone rang.

"Altair, Altair," came an excited voice. "You'll never guess what happened."

"I probably won't. Who is this?"

And the Mom who had tried to get Altair to help her son told him this story.

"Well, he did what you told him. He meditated on the problem and the solution and then handed it all over to God. Then just as you suggested he called ten movie producers in Hollywood including the numbers you gave him."

Altair had recently returned from Hollywood and passed on some contacts in the movie industry that he knew there to the woman's son.

"The first nine said no. When my son got to the tenth he was starting to feel dejected. He still went ahead with the call as you suggested. The secretary to the producer was very kind, took his number, as he was calling from a friend's house, and said she would call back if there were any auditions coming up that he might be interested in. Only a matter of a minute or so later there was a call.

"Hello is this Allan?" said the voice.

"Yes."

"I happened to be in the office and overheard your call. Would you mind retelling me what you related to my secretary?"

My son told his story all over again. The movie producer was so touched he invited Allan down to visit him in Hollywood when his health was better!"

Three years later Allan's mom contacted Altair again. She told him the follow up to the phone call. The producer gave her son an audition for a small part in an up-and-coming play. Then he flew the family down and had them stay in his own private apartments while they got settled. Now Allan is happily based in Hollywood as an actor earning a reasonable salary and living his dream.

These were messages from the angel for Altair.

He was being given more and more signs that the conscious universe was communicating to him.

The numbers of people who sought him out for advice became quite overwhelming, so he sought his own advice from a medical intuitive named Sita. She was employed by hospitals in difficult-to-diagnose cases as she could look into a patient's body and see where the trauma was.

"Oh," she said the moment she met him. "You're a *Naga*!"

Altair looked her straight in the eyes.

"You see? You know how to manipulate the energies, you're doing it right now. You can weave the matrix that exists right across the cosmos and tap into its energies. You can see people's place in it and help awaken them to it."

It was true. Altair had been visited by a number of psychics and spiritual healers all who wanted to go deeper in their experiences. He only had to look into their eyes and raise his own energy and whatever experience they were desiring would be granted instantaneously. It was all to do with the fire of bliss in the inner spine that God or Spirit activated through him when he connected with people by touch or by gaze.

"But be careful," she cautioned. "The *Naga* energy or serpent Fire is very hypnotic and can lead to enormous trouble with the opposite sex. You must be very careful about your boundaries with people or your relationships will be destroyed."

Altair knew this already. The power of the inner fire often activated powerful sexuality mixed in with love so had to be dealt with very sensitively. Altair had spent time in many communities where the leader, often a male, at some point was involved in sexual misconduct and Altair was left to help counsel the many angry devotees.

"The *Naga* is an ancient energy. You can wield powers that may seem miraculous to ordinary folk."

Altair had witnessed many miracles merely by him saying that a person would receive healing or abundance or love if they had faith. He had visited a wonderful man called Bart in Ashland who had been a fighter pilot in the war.

"I was shot down over the ocean," said Bart, "and when I bailed I landed near a Japanese freighter whose men opened fire on me with machine guns. I sustained shrapnel wounds in my spine and was left for dead in the water for many hours until a rescue crew found me. I've had this pain in my back and legs for years and can hardly walk."

"Lie on the bed," said Altair, "and we'll see what we can do."

Altair worked on Bart's legs and back for two hours, sometimes praying, sometimes laying hands on, and sometimes using a combination of acupressure and shiatsu touch points. By the time he left, Bart was fast asleep.

The next morning, he received a phone call from a Californian TV station.

"Hello, is this Altair?"

"Yes."

"We have a gentleman here called Bart who claims you healed him."

"Healed? He's healed?"

"Yes, he says he has had bad pain in his back and legs for years and that you came like an angel and touched him, and he was healed."

Altair was silent. The angel's hand at work again.

"My name's Joan," said the voice. "I'm the producer for the show. Would you mind coming down to the studios? We'd like to interview you."

Altair told Aria and together they went to the TV studios. Altair told his story and they sang together on air and were promoted across California as the singers who heal the heart.

That pretty much summed up Altair's mission, an earth angel who heals the heart.

Altair looked at Sita. Sita was beautiful and fierce-eyed, and now he saw something different. He was looking straight into the eyes of another *Naga*. Her cheeks flushed as he met her gaze and his heart quickened as he felt the familiar rush of energies in his spine.

In her place, it was the Dalai Lama speaking to him.

"Your brain, your heart is your temple. Look there for what you seek. Let your path be love and kindness."

Some years ago, Altair had sponsored the Dalai Lama's first trip to New Zealand and had been fortunate enough to meet His Holiness for a private audience. Then, as in all their meetings, whenever he asked about Avalokiteshvara Guan Yin, the Goddess of Compassion, the Dalai Lama would say to him,

"Study, and then practice being Avalokiteshvara by being love and kindness and compassion for all people in your heart. Then teach ten people and ask them to teach ten more and ask them to do the same and so on until this entire world is transformed and liberated through your loving kindness. Then you will have successfully transformed yourself and all others into Avalokiteshvara."

Now the Dalai Lama transformed back into Sita and then again into Guan Yin.

"Just as two of the Buddha's disciples are Great *Naga* and hold *naga*-jewels or Chintamani Stones, so you who are *Naga* will find your own *naga*-jewel in My Heart."

Then Guan Yin gathered Altair into Her own heart and flew with him to Her celestial palace in the Pure Land on Mount Potalaka, where beings of every kind from many worlds came to seek Her Wisdom and Compassion. Altair could see monks and nuns, making their way through the Goddess Tara's Rosewood Forest, seeking rebirth on Potalaka and even more who had come to seek the advice of the Bodhisattva Avalokiteshvara Guan Yin. The passes on the mountain were very dangerous, its sides precipitous and its valleys rugged. On the top of the mountain was a lake, its waters as clear as a mirror. From the grotto flowed a great river which encircled the mountain and flowed down to the southern sea. The celestial palace lay beside the lake. Rare medicinal herbs grew in its gardens and exquisite lotus flowers bloomed in small ponds. Lions, elephants, horses, peacocks, and garuda roamed the larger garden areas, all in the peace and bliss of the presence of Guan Yin.

The vision vanished, and Altair was sitting still facing Sita.

"To cross the bridge between worlds takes great love and compassion," said Sita. "You never take the trip alone. Because to succeed you need to free humanity of its fear and suffering. That is what we are all here to do, together."

Altair travelled up and down the west coast of the United States and Canada bringing healing, love and compassion before he returned to the Deep South and then Australia. Of all the wonders he could imagine it is often the simplest things that bring the deepest joy. He was reunited with his childhood friend Hannah in Sydney and he, Aria and Hannah and her partner Isaac all settled in the same suburb in Sydney right near the beach. Every morning Altair swam, occasionally brushing up against tiger sharks and man-o-war jellyfish, not without incident especially one day when he was stung badly by a jellyfish and had to spend three days in bed, unable to walk.

While he was looking for work Hannah introduced him to Jennifer, a Sai Baba devotee and very wealthy millionaire who had made her money in the property market.

"How would you like to run a health clinic for people here in Sydney?" asked Jennifer one day out of the blue.

"I have the money to fund it and Sai Baba came to me in a dream and told me that you are the person to run it."

As simple as that, Altair found himself running a clinic with doctors, massage therapists, Chinese acupuncturists, astrologers, and counselors all bringing health and healing to the public.

He was fortunate enough to meet the great Reiki Master Dr. Premaratna and train with him in healing and awakening through the Reiki Jin Kei Do system which comes directly from a lineage of Indian, Tibetan and Shingon Buddhism healing methods.

It was on one of those health and healing days, very close to the clinic where he practiced with Dr. Premaratna, that Sai Baba acted again in Altair's life, in the most mysterious way.

Altair was walking in the local shopping area with Aria, when a woman walking past stopped them.

"Sai Baba wants you to come and visit him at my sacred shrine. He has a gift for you. He has been waiting for you."

"Sai Baba is a Messenger from God," said Altair.

The woman nodded and gave them her card.

"My name is Shanti. I will see you at 5."

So that afternoon, Altair and Aria went to a house just above the beach and knocked on the door.

The same woman who had met them earlier bowed and let them in.

"Follow me," she said.

They went with her down into her basement where there were two statues, both sitting in pools of what at first appeared to be water.

The first statue was of Ganesha, the god of good fortune, remover of obstacles, patron of the arts, sciences and wisdom.

Out of his trunk poured a golden nectar for which Altair could see no obvious source.

Shanti pointed to the large bowl that was overflowing now with the liquid which dripped onto plastic sheets on the floor.

"Taste it," she said. "Nectar from Heaven, Amrita, the Ambrosia of Immortality. To taste it is to attain higher knowledge and power."

Altair did taste it and it was sweet, not like honey or sugar but a different sweetness altogether with the lightness and glow of heaven.

Then he turned to the second statue.

It was a statue of Guan Yin.

"Kneel down and pray to Her," said Shanti. "If She is willing and you touch Her Heart with compassion She will give you a priceless gift."

He looked at Guan Yin and She looked at him and he finally understood what Manjushri and Sai Baba had said, that he would find the Chintamani Stone in the Heart of Guan Yin.

Altair knelt and prayed. He knew he had been waiting for this moment for a long time.

"Hold out your hands," said Shanti.

As Altair held out his hands, cupped, under the Heart of Guan Yin's statue, the most amazing miracle occurred. From the Heart of Guan Yin, the most beautiful pearl began to grow. It emerged little by little, like a baby from the womb of Her Heart. To his amazement, as the head of the pearl and then the body appeared, he saw the beautiful pearl was attached by a thin strand of pearl silk to the statue's heart, like a baby's umbilical cord to its mother. Gradually the weight of the pearl allowed the silk strand to stretch and lower the pearl and eventually to break off in Altair's hands.

"You must be a monk," said Shanti. "When I travelled to see Sai Baba, he guided me to a monastery in Sri Lanka where his monks had prayed over this statue for years. They gave me the statue and said to use it to heal the world. They said it had great powers of manifestation and miracles and would recognize a monk by the power of his compassionate heart and give him a Chintamani Stone accordingly."

Altair's eyes filled with tears of gratitude.

He bowed deeply to Guan Yin and gave deep and reverent thanks for this miracle.

CHAPTER 10

Kalachakra

Altair sat quietly beside the mirror lake in the Deep South near the Alps watching the stars as they whirled across the sky, mirrored in the still waters. Time had passed, stars had set, suns rose, and Altair was dreaming again. Aria and Altair had travelled the world and created the most magnificent music, yet here he was, again on his own, filled with a profound sadness. He heard the murmur of a storm, in the hills beyond the lake and in the caves of his heart, because all was not well in the ebb and flow of his life. Twice already he and Aria had separated, and this third time seemed destined to be for good. The Sanyasi's message in India had once again proven correct. The 16th century Raj and his wives were still living out their karma through Altair.

Altair spoke to the lake and the hills and the sky.

"What part am I supposed to play? How can I understand the powers at play in love?"

And a Voice came to him from beyond the Stars.

"Put an end to Karma. Turn the Wheel of Time."

"An end? The Wheel of Time?"

There was no answer. Just the rumbling of the storm and some lightning flashes in the far-off hills.

The wheel of time. The Dalai Lama had mentioned something to him once. The Wheel of Time. The Kalachakra. So had Manjushri.

It did not make any sense to Altair right now. But it would soon.

Because right at that moment in another country, as the sun was rising, Padma awoke.

She was a dreamer, like Altair.

And that night she had dreamed a strange dream.

It was the most auspicious night of the year to dream a dream in Japan, January 2nd. In Japanese culture, *Hatsuyume* (初夢) is the first dream you have in the new year. Traditionally, the contents of such a dream would foretell the luck of the dreamer in the ensuing year.

Padma dreamed of a man with curly hair, a stranger from a strange land. He was married with children and he was her destiny. Where she would meet him, she didn't know. She got up and made herself some toast and coffee, still puzzled by the dream. She had made an appointment to meet a friend later that morning and then she would go to the travel office to book a holiday in the Deep South near the Alps.

"The wheel of time? The Kalachakra?" Altair sat twirling his fingers in the cold waters of the lake. He remembered what Manjushri had said to him,

"I can grant you universal sight, and the first sign will be when you are given a real Chintamani Stone, a Pearl of Light, manifested from the Heart of Guan Yin. You have been an acolyte of the Bodhisattva Avalokiteshvara Guan Yin, which is why you are attracted to the teachings of the Dalai Lama, whom you died defending in 1959. The second sign will be when you have a direct experience of the Pure Light of Being through the Kalachakra Tantra with the Dalai Lama."

The first sign had been given, a Pearl, from the Heart of Guan Yin. The second was to experience the Pure Light of Being, through the Dalai Lama. Like all signs, Altair trusted in the flow to bring it to him in the right time and the right place.

Altair made some notes for his new book, 'Startribes' before he returned to his car.

'The stars and magic. End Karma. Kalachakra, Dalai Lama. Follow your dreams.'

The book seemed to be writing itself. He had just been given a new contract with a UK publisher. The main character, Altair, a traveler of the stars was about to meet a girl who had the power of a Violet Star. He had been wondering what he should name her.

It suddenly dawned on him.

He would name her Padma.

Padma, who lived near Tokyo in Japan, had decided to go on a working holiday to the Deep South. She booked a ski and snowboard holiday with a school that also taught English. She needed to brush up on her skills before she took up a job as a tour guide or something similar that could use her previous experience with the airlines. She used to work as a VIP escort for celebrities like fashion models, actresses, and musicians at the international airport. Perhaps her curly-headed dream man was a musician too.

Altair took the elevator to the top floor of the lakefront hotel. As manager of the ski and snowboard school in the winter, he often had to pick up groups from the airport. He had a pickup in about an hour. The woman who said she wanted to meet him gave no details. Just that they would meet on the top floor. He got out and looked around. The hotel had wonderful marble details and plush decor of red, gold and wooden trim. There was no one there. Altair hesitated and then turned to leave.

"Hello Altair," said a voice.

As Altair turned back a woman stood up from one of the lounge areas. Perhaps she had been sitting there all along and he hadn't noticed. She looked like she had just emerged from the ocean. Her ash-blonde hair was braided and filled with seashell clips and starfish accessories and her face was deeply tanned as if she'd just stepped off a sailing boat. Her dress was sea-blue, and she wore matching lapis and emerald jewelry on her neck and wrists. Her beach sandals were pure white, almost the same color as her hair. She had deep blue eyes which sparkled with delight and mischief.

"Thank you for meeting me," she said with still no introduction.

"And you are …" said Altair, fishing for her name.

"A Messenger."

"From Sai Baba?" Altair figured it was worth a guess.

"I wish," she said with a laugh. "No, I just bring you a simple message from the ones that sent me. Follow your dreams. Remember the language of Love. I think you are about to get a call from her."

"Her?" said Altair. His mobile rang at that very moment.

"Hello?"

"Hi, Altair. It's Liam here." Liam, the owner of the ski and snowboard and English school. No 'her' about him.

"I forgot to tell you who you are picking up. A Japanese girl named Padma. She sometimes goes by the name of Violet."

Altair was speechless.

"Altair?"

"Yes, fine," Altair said when he found his voice. "I'm on my way."

"By the way, she's here already. Her flight was diverted to Invercargill and then she caught a bus to the school."

Altair turned back to the woman.

"How did you know about her?"

But there was no one there.

When Altair met Padma he instantly knew his destiny had changed. He didn't know how it would change or what their future would be. He only knew he had found a friend forever.

Padma thought Altair had the brightest, most radiant smile, like the sun. She loved the ski and snowboard school. She especially liked Altair, who seemed to know how to put her at ease. One day they were out in a group that Altair was guiding on the mountain. He skied, and she snowboarded. She was feeling tired that day so halfway down the slope she started to fall behind the group, so she turned the snowboard right off the slope and lay down in the soft snow, looking up at the sky. A moment later she felt the snow shift and Altair slid in beside her and lay on the snow and looked up at the sky. With one voice they said,

"What a beautiful blue sky."

And then they knew.

At the time of Padma's farewell from the ski and snowboard school, she wrote a poem for Altair which she read out to the group.

"Being with you is like a hot spring."

And then the whole group knew.

Altair and Padma travelled for a while in the group together. They travelled in the front of a large van which Altair drove, with another friend, Kumi. At these moments time stood still, and Altair realized the power of the words "Turn the wheel of time." Something was happening. They were entering a timeless zone together in which all language and all experience was One. They both called this their love language, a language capable of crossing the bridge between worlds and touching the stars with magic. Even in a crowd of people, they could talk about any subject and it would take on the cadence of a musical duet and enchant those around them so that everything else faded into a dream and only love existed. Love language is an alchemical language and as they were about to discover can transform the human world into an enchanted one or even cross dimensions into Pure Lands.

One weekend they travelled with a group of tourists to one of the main glaciers in the Deep South. The trip was long and covered walking through forested regions as well as along the glacier itself, which involved a short trek to get to the foot of the ice river.

As the group walked they became split until there was a group ahead and another behind with Altair and Padma in the middle.

"Let's stop here," said Altair as they paused beside a break in the path. They couldn't see the forward group or the back one as they were standing on a bend with a small fork heading off to their right.

"Where are we?" asked Padma.

"I don't know," said Altair. "I've been here before, but I don't recognize this fork." He unfolded the map he was carrying and peered at it. "And I don't see it marked here either."

"Let's catch the others up," said Padma.

"Let's not," laughed Altair. "I want to explore."

Leading the way, Altair made his way down the narrow path which turned left and then right through a narrow copse of trees.

Suddenly he stopped. He drew in his breath and pointed ahead.

"Oh, my goodness!"

Padma stood alongside him and took his hand in hers.

There, in magnificent glory sprawled the most exquisite garden Altair and Padma had ever laid their eyes upon. It glowed with a freshness and vitality unknown on earth, a mystical enchanted garden that should be inhabited by fairies and elves.

"It's a *Rakuen*," said Padma. "I never believed it was possible to see one in my lifetime."

"*Rakuen?*" said Altair.

"*Rakuen* is Japanese for paradise, an enchanted garden, one you might find in fairytales. How is this possible?"

"The language of love," said Altair. "That is what makes it possible."

Padma nodded.

"Somehow love crosses the bridge across forever," said Altair, "and brings into being the dreams of myth and fantasy."

The garden was a truly extraordinary mix of mountain meadow and highland springs with gorgeous flowers and shrubs dotted amongst the verdant trees. Everything glowed with an aura of emerald light, and just to be present there was to drink in the nectar of heaven itself, it was so rejuvenating.

They tried to use the cameras to take photos, but the electronics weren't working.

After they had drunk their fill of this richness of life Altair and Padma turned back to the main path and continued up the track until they reached the group, not so far ahead after all.

"Sorry to keep you all waiting," said Altair.

"We took a detour," said Padma.

"Sorry?" said Luke, one of the tour leaders. "What for? We saw you stop on the bend back there and then head off into the bush. We thought you must have stopped for a kiss." Everyone laughed. "Didn't take long," he added with a grin.

"Long?" said Altair puzzled. "No, we found a garden, an amazing garden, back down there. I'm sure we were gone for at least half an hour."

He could see the bewilderment on the others' faces.

"Look I'll show you on the way back."

He marked the spot where they were now as the bend was only 50m or so back the way they had come.

After visiting the glacier and taking photos Altair and Padma were still on a high from their *Rakuen* experience. When he got to the mark Altair proudly said, "Now we'll show you something to remember."

But when they got to the bend a little further on they found nothing. No *Rakuen*, no fork in the path, only dense impenetrable underbrush.

They never found the *Rakuen* again.

"The love language is like a secret key to forgotten places," said Altair.

"Are you the one who is doing all this?" said Padma. She still couldn't believe what she had experienced.

"I think the bridge across forever is opened by very simple pure acts of love and compassion. Like the angel and the homeless girl. That is the way to turn the wheel of time."

"To put an end to karma?"

"Yes, I feel that is what we are supposed to be doing."

"Bringing love and compassion."
"Love, compassion and wisdom."

One day Altair and Padma went further south on the east coast to Whale Beach. It was a very isolated place, that very few tourists ever visited. Altair had told Padma about the signs and she had witnessed the pearl's healing power for herself when she was sick. Altair's connection to the Divine Mother, Guan Yin, seemed to have the ability to heal her pain immediately. The pearl heightened that power. He also showed her some of the power of the second sign, the Kalachakra, which he had begun studying. He told Padma about Shambhala as they were walking over the fields and pastures towards the beach.

"Shambhala is a beacon of hope for so many people," said Altair. "It is a pure land, beyond the reach of ordinary travelers, a land that only appears to those of great merit. Through making prayer-wishes some can be reborn or even visit Shambhala so as to enjoy the continual teaching of the Kalachakra. In 2425 there will be a great war in which Maitreya will return and all fear will be defeated. Then the universal teaching of love and light and compassion will flourish upon the earth."

As Altair was talking to Padma they reached an old farm gate. It looked rickety and old and would have to be climbed with care.

Suddenly they both stood stock still.

"What's that light?"

They both felt simultaneously an enormous energy wave of love pass through them and uplift them.

Altair saw a gleam of light and first a stream and then a torrent of golden light struck them from the source of Shambhala itself.

Surrounding Altair and Padma were golden bodhisattvas and angels gazing down at them. They formed a golden halo, a circle of radiance, which to this day Altair called "The Golden Wave". Padma felt a vibration, warm and pulsing like an ocean current, going right through her body and passing up the inside of her spine, an angel of healing from another world.

The Circle of Light then passed around, through and over them both, first moving like lightning flashes across the ocean and then taking to the skies, flying into and beyond the stars as One.

Padma was shocked.

"What was that?"

Altair understood how she felt. To touch another world was to throw all you knew into deep confusion. It was a wordless timeless gift from beyond. He knew the light beings gathered when something precious like the language of love was truly being expressed through two people here on earth. He could see how people from all over the world would travel to be close to something so special and how they would learn to activate it within themselves. The I AM Presence. The Power of God within, common to all faiths and beliefs and religions. He knew then that he was closer than close to the Pure Light of Being and that love and compassion and wisdom was the key. Altair and Padma saw pure rarefied beauty and light that day, and that feeling would never leave them.

CHAPTER 11

Avalon

"Dream deeper," said the stars. "Dream higher," said the magic.

Altair dreamed with Padma, that they could cross the bridge across forever with the language of love. They were travelers of destiny and their journey was to be filled with deep valleys and steep slopes and some very rocky passes.

The road to Avalon began some years before on a basketball court in California as the sun set low in a beautiful azure sky. Altair was playing with two other friends.

"Altair, you're much better at rugby!" said Andy.

"I know. I played netball in the Deep South, not … hey!!!"

A raccoon hurtled across the court out of the forest that bordered one end, hit Altair in the legs then hit the notice board at the other end before hightailing it back into the forest.

"What was that?" said Tom.

"So weird," said Andy. "I've never seen a raccoon act like that."

"Like it was trying to send me a message," said Altair, "the way it hit me, then the notice board, to make sure I wouldn't miss it."

"What is that on the board anyway?" said Andy pointing to a solitary notice that fluttered in the breeze.

Altair walked over and read it out loud.

"Tareth. Western Sai Baba. 8 pm. By donation only. Oh, it's in the church. Over there tonight."

He pointed to a small church which backed onto a hall, halfway embedded in the forest the raccoon had emerged from.

"Anyone going?"

"Nah," said Andy.

"Doesn't interest me," said Tom.

"I might go," said Altair.

"Sounds like your sort of thing Altair," said Tom.

"Wouldn't surprise me if you were long lost brothers or something," said Andy.

'Wouldn't surprise me either', thought Altair. He had that strange unnerving feeling in his stomach that something unusual was about to happen and that he had been specifically guided here to this very place at this very particular time.

Altair entered the small church at about 8 o'clock. There was a gathering of about 50 people all facing a man seated in a chair who was facing them. Everything was silent and still. There was no noise, so Altair sat in the second row and watched. Then another man with ash-white hair wearing dark sunglasses came in from a side door. Altair felt instant recognition. A group just like this, sitting around something very precious, in ancient times. He could scarcely breathe. The air around him began to shimmer and he could have sworn he heard some sounds, like a crystal chime, something altogether unearthly. The sun-glassed man held his hands above the seated man's head and as Altair watched dark ash began to drop, flakes at a time, out of those hands. Altair's heart began to ache as if he was longing for something.

"I am here for you," said a voice.

Altair turned around, the voice seemed to come from his left shoulder, but no one was there.

"Auriel?" Altair was sure it was the angelic presence, guiding him. No answer.

Altair looked again at the man wearing sunglasses.

"Father?" said Altair without thinking. The feeling was gone before Altair could continue. Altair was about to reach for the stars with some new magic.

After the demonstration which included healing oil that the man with sunglasses, Tareth, was able to manifest directly from his hands, Altair asked to see him privately. They made an appointment immediately after the healing ceremony and he met with Tareth in a back room. It was close and intimate, so he could feel Tareth's vibration more clearly.

He looked across at Tareth. Tareth's hands were loosely draped in his lap, his face pale against Altair's own tanned skin.

"Do you know my origins?" asked Altair. "I had an experience where a friend and I were able to call a starcraft."

"You are from the stars, Altair. Like me. The Pleiades. You carry the magic of the stars in the temple of your heart."

Tareth reached out to Altair and took his hands.

The instant they touched there was a pulse-like electricity which burst through Altair's body and exploded in his heart. Altair felt like he had developed a new sense altogether, the bliss sense, where joy was much more in focus than ever before. His mission to liberate others through awakening this same joy in their hearts was quite simply now very close and very real.

At that moment a voice from across time reached out and called to him.

"Emrys Myrddin."

The explosion of joy was filling him with vision.

Altair looked up from the long Grail Crystal that lay between him and Tareth that he had been saying enchantments over.

"I can see people approaching. Shall we conceal this?"

It was Tareth but not as he looked now. As the leader of the Merlin Source Group, he was often hidden with spells of invisibility and concealment so that no one would see him as he worked his magic with the group.

"Keep it hidden, keep it safe, seal it." said one of the members of the Source Group that Altair could see encircling the crystal. They stood together over an underground alchemic temple.

The group began to emit sounds of different harmonic frequencies through their bodies. It was most unusual to meet any alchemist when they chanted like this with their chakras wide open as the sound filled the air with eerie, otherworldly melodies. The sounds were the key to opening the inter-dimensional doors, which would conceal and then hold the energy of the Grail Crystal until it was time to be released.

The alchemists knelt down low and pressed their palms upon the ground. A hole appeared in the earth. In the distance, a group of mounted knights approached. The alchemists, when they reached a certain frequency pushed their hands holding the crystal, which they named "the sword in the stone" deep into the earth, their arms sinking into the hole in the ground right up to their shoulders.

"The wisdom is in the earth," Altair repeated quietly with the others. The Grail Crystal was hidden just before the Knights came upon them.

The leader of the riders wore a golden helmet and rode a fierce white charger. He did not dismount.

He stopped by the water's edge and held his sword up in salute.

"We have come for Merlin," he said.

"On whose order?" It was a woman in Tareth's group who spoke.

"Morgan Le Fay."

Altair shuddered. He had never felt quite so cold as he did right now.

Three men stepped forward from the Merlin group, none of them Tareth.

"We are Merlin."

The Golden-helmeted rider edged his horse up to the nearest man, swung his sword and decapitated him at the neck.

"You are next," he pointed his sword at the second Merlin, "unless you hand over Merlin."

Altair at that moment wanted to fight the golden warrior, but some good fortune held him back and instead he focused on chanting a new spell. A spell of dissolution. He began to breathe in the inner spine and tone internally, reaching out into the silence.

"Priests and priestesses," laughed the Warrior. "Weak and helpless fools against Mordred."

"Avalon will never kneel to traitors," said the second man, and Mordred in a rage at this defiance rode the man through with his sword. The dead man slumped to his knees held aloft on Mordred's sword.

"Now who is kneeling," laughed Mordred again. It was a harsh merciless laugh with not the faintest hint of remorse.

"I will kill all of you," said Mordred.

"No, you won't," said Tareth as he stepped forward. "I will come with you."

Altair's heart lurched in dismay. He couldn't let them take his father. He knew Morgan's reputation. She would take all she wanted from Tareth and then dispose of him.

"A wise decision," said Mordred. "But first I want to know why my mother desires you so."

"Simple," said Tareth. "I have the love and wisdom she needs to complete her training."

"Love and wisdom? Are you as foolish as your followers?" Mordred rode his horse forward until it was standing on one of the dead bodies. "I can give your people fear and suffering in their ignorance of the truth. You are no more than a puppet, just like your master Arthur."

"He is not my Master."

"Whom do you serve?"

"The Source."

"Serve me. I can give you more than any source. You could be useful."

"You don't fool me, Morgan. Reveal yourself."

Instantly the helmeted figure on the horse dissolved to reveal a graceful red-haired young woman surrounded not by Knights but by eight equally vivacious women. The nine sisters of Avalon.

"Oh, why can't you play my games," she smiled leaning off her horse to stroke Tareth's cheek. "I only want to know a little more of your magic."

"Take me," said Tareth, "I'll do what you want."

"Oh, you'll do what I want," said Morgan. "And I can make sure your little tricks don't go unrewarded." She stroked a hand down the length of his chin and ran her fingers through his beard. "You know I can please you more than this."

Altair wanted to shout at Tareth. But he should have known better. As Morgan wrapped her arm slowly around Tareth's neck and shoulders, Tareth slipped his arm around her waist and pulled her hard off her horse.

Altair watched, curious to see what Tareth would do next. Altair stood still and silent and calm. He had finished the spell of dissolution and it began to work. He felt the grove of trees around them that extended down to the lakeside on the island shimmer and shiver and then shift into the walls of the room he had entered to see Tareth earlier on that evening.

Tareth was still holding Altair's hands but now something different was happening. The joy in Altair's heart began to move down his arms and into his hands as if he too, like the spell, was dissolving.

Oil, aromatic oil and a nectar, like the Amrita of Ganesha he had tasted, began to flood out of Altair's heart and down his arms into his hands. It started to drip, drip, drip and then rush like a small stream. It wouldn't stop.

"Could I have some paper towels?" he asked Tareth with embarrassment.

Tareth had an assistant who left immediately and returned bringing some towels and some plastic vials.

"You may want to collect it," said Tareth. "The divine oil is just an example of the many miracles contained in the temple of your heart."

The oil flowed from Altair's hands for over eight hours. In that time, he visited many friends with massage practices and they collected the oil for use with their clients.

Altair stayed in touch with Tareth over many years. He introduced Padma to the sounds he called the Yeshua Codes as well as the Shambhala Codes he received through Tareth.

"What is it?" exclaimed Padma the first time she listened. "It vibrates in every part of my body. It's like the sound is living in my cells."

"I know what you mean," said Altair. "They are the sounds we used in Merlin's time to bury wisdom artifacts, just like the *terma* of Tibet that Padmasambhava and Yeshe Tsogyal hid in the ground so that these treasures could be discovered at a later time. They are wisdom teachings, encoded in the sounds. When I worked with them again, just before I played them to you, the sounds manifested in our lounge here, sounding like a sputnik transiting across the room from the left to the right."

"What does Tareth do? What do the sounds do really?"

"The harmonic frequencies open inter-dimensional portals. They give us access to other worlds, planets and stars in our galaxy and beyond, as well as other dimensional worlds. It is easier to access these portals at earth energy centers, which are the real doorways for communication, places like Stonehenge, Jerusalem, Varanasi, Giza, Macchu Picchu, Uluru, Sedona, and Glastonbury. The true Grail is within the Temple of the Heart and these energy centers help us to find that energy more easily and awaken it."

There was a movement in the room. Altair gave a soft shiver.

"Do you feel it?"

"What is it?" Padma's hairs on the back of her neck stood on end.

Altair knew the energy immediately.

"Auriel," he whispered.

"Ah," said Padma, "the angel and the homeless girl."

"The sounds will open any door, even the path to angels," smiled Altair through soft tears.

That night as Padma fell fast asleep, Altair was lying on the bed, gazing at the ceiling, when the room was filled with a beautiful light. In front of Altair's eyes, the whole room was transformed into a strange new world, that he could best describe as having x-ray vision into the splendor of inter-dimensional worlds.

Waves of joy filled Altair as Auriel appeared and guided him through world after world.

"Child," said Auriel.

"Auriel," whispered Altair from deep inside his heart, "why did you not return sooner after I met the homeless girl in America?" He did not have to speak out loud. The thoughts were transmitted instantly to Auriel.

"I am the archangel of wisdom and the arts," said Auriel, reminding Altair of Saraswati. "You have much to learn on your own. I did not want to interfere."

Altair looked into the space above him. A Flower of Life appeared less than a metre from his head as real and solid as if someone was holding an enormous sunflower there. He reached out to touch it in disbelief.

"Behold, this is a portal, manifest. You see it as real, although it is created by dream yoga. Your own body that you feel as so real is a dream body. I am a protector of this planet but not from this planet, from one very similar to yours."

Altair's own body felt lighter as if he could begin to move freely.

"Can I travel through there?"

"Just as you can walk and move on earth, so can angelic forces move throughout universes to assist those in other illumined planets. I help those who have developed deeply spiritually in other realms to attain liberation. All those I help are free like you feel now, and can consciously leave their bodies at death and move into the light body state.

Most humans on earth pass from earth to other dimensional spheres, where they work to fully free their souls from all traces of karma. Some come from subtle dimensions beyond that, close to Source or God and return to assist all into liberation. This is the ultimate act of compassion.

Each dimension is subtler than the last. On earth you are aware of the physical senses, when you let go of the body you work with the energy of consciousness and a body composed of varying degrees not of matter but of *prana* or life force. When you free yourself of that you are able to be in the energy of bliss and the bliss body.

Come fly with me."

Altair felt himself lift up and free himself of his body and enter the Flower of Life. Each petal glowed like a separate dream world which Altair found he could enter at will.

"There are many worlds like this one," said Auriel as they travelled in an arc through one such dimension. It was not like seeing with normal sight. Altair could actually feel the life force of numerous worlds at once and see through them as if they were made of masses of light moving with different laws of physics that made perceiving them an extraordinary shift for the senses.

"These dimensions are subtle vibrations of the light and sound you find on earth. The enormous power you are feeling is because these worlds are many times greater than the physical universe. The dimensions you perceive with consciousness and *prana* are like rainbow worlds, with so many more degrees of refinement than the physical ones. Many of the myths and legends of fairies, dragons and deities come from these subtler dimensions. Just as there are battles amongst humans filled with fear and ignorance on earth, so there are wars in a subtler way played out here amongst fallen angels, working out their misguided karma. The divine will is crucial here. On earth, humans are only fleetingly aware of it, but here it is the basis of the play of consciousness and *prana*. Everything is attuned to that divine will and on the worlds you are perceiving, beings use grace to create. The movement and shifts experienced on these worlds can be created at will by a truly advanced being.

The divine will is channeled through the subtle center in what used to be the physical brain, a thousand-petaled lotus of light and through the astral spine or *sushumna* which you have learned to access through Kriya Yoga. Through the power of light and sound in these subtle centers you call *chakras*, the beings of these worlds can shift and change shape through *pranic* or energy practices. This is why knowledge of the sacred breath is so important while in the physical body on earth.

The most important sense to develop on earth in conjunction with the breath is the sixth sense of intuition. Your physical world in time will recognize the value of going beyond the five senses and will set up schools of training in intuition which is how all beings on the subtle worlds communicate. Many of the earth practices such as Tai Chi, yoga, meditation and alchemy assist the physical development of intuition so that the third eye is naturally wide awake when you leave the physical body behind on earth at the transition you call death. The *pranic* body of consciousness perceives just as you are doing right now, directly through intuition. Healing is done instantly by attunement to the divine will because there is no longer any attachment to a physical body.

The power of *mudra*, which are ritual gestures, *mantra* or sacred sounds, and *mandala* and *yantra* or sacred symbols is particularly important on earth to access the power of consciousness in the subtle realms. *Thangka* or paintings of light, source codes or sounds of divine origin and ancient and modern symbols such as OM are actually manifestations of *pranic* consciousness which can be used on earth as portals to access the timeless realm.

Not all humans have been trained to use the sounds from their body like you did in Avalon and the way Tareth manifests now, so anyone can use sacred sounds to make the journey, much like shamans have done since ancient times, if they develop presence.

There are many portals to presence, the subtle realms and Pure Lands. The simplest is mindfulness. Deep visualizations on feeling the inner body as pure energy, consciousness or bliss and light can liberate you directly into the formless realm. Sitting still and noticing the silence, the stillness and presence that follows as you listen deeply and notice the silence, also liberates you. Who is noticing the silence? The I AM Presence. Noticing the silence frees you of thought. Thoughts are like waves on the ocean. You see the waves, the thoughts of this world but do not identify with them. To be in this world and yet not be of it is the key. To go about your daily activities aware of the stillness within even while you engage in life keeps the portal to presence open and allows you to walk in the Pure Lands even as you walk on the earth, with practice. Stillness in motion.

Surrendering your self, silence, stillness, and emptiness all are paths to the unknown, to a shift to pure consciousness. We surround our self constantly with movement, noise, and filling in all available spaces in our schedules, almost totally unaware of the vastness of Being that makes up everything else in existence.

When we look at ourselves we see that the things we are concerned with make up such a very small amount of this world and that the world is an incredibly tiny part of All That Is, which includes 100 billion galaxies we do not know about and all the multiple dimensions that exist within and alongside those. What we are concerned with is very small, a tiny part of the known, and we live in fear of the unknown. We never know God because we make up religions and images which support a limited distorted vision of how great God really is, and that God is both within and all around us and far beyond.

The stillness and silence that is the portal to God is not out there somewhere but within us," said Auriel. "'Be still and know God' from Psalm 46:10 tells us the truth. When you are truly present, then there is presence and that portal will open you to God's Light, Source, the Buddha within you, that has been there all along. You are here to enable the divine within you to unfold."

CHAPTER 12

Shambhala 2425

"You will have a child."

"Auriel said that to you?"

"Yes, a girl. Then a boy if their destiny matches."

"What does that mean?" asked Padma. She wasn't so sure about giving birth let alone have two kids. Birth seemed so painful.

"I've always wanted to give birth," said Altair. "I must have been a mother more than once."

"I'm happy to let you do it," said Padma with a smile. "If you can figure out the issue with your anatomy!" she said pointing to his jeans. "Did Auriel say anything else?"

"Just that she would be the mother."

"Who? Our daughter?"

"Yes."

"I'm not sure I like the sound of that. You want to be one, she's going to be one and I'm one giving birth to a mother!"

Altair laughed.

"Mother of Dragons. Mother of Storms. She can be mother of lots of things."

From his practice of awakening the divine within Altair could see this child awakening very early.

He sent a soul call to her guides to bring the child to them when the time was right. Then he focused on his early morning Kalachakra ritual and called to the Bodhisattvas, Archangels and Elders.

"From my heart, I go for refuge to the three jewels, Buddha Dharma Sangha, Christ Krishna, Divine Mother. I will free all beings from pain and set all in final bliss. To do that I will generate an altruistic intention to attain perfect enlightenment and thereupon train in the learnings of Bodhisattvas, Archangels and Elders."

Altair had headed down to the beach after one of these practices in the early morning. The temperature had dropped, and he lay down next to Cave Rock to watch the ocean. The seabirds were swirling in the breeze and the terns were calmly searching for shellfish in the shallows. Altair was waiting for Sam with whom he had promised to do some martial arts sparring and wrestling. Sam was several sizes larger than Altair and a lot stronger, but Altair was much faster, so he thought he was in with a chance. It was all for fun anyway and a good way to keep fit. He put his hand up to rub his left shoulder which he had dislocated numerous times in adrenaline sports like kayaking and abseiling, so he knew he had to be careful.

Altair wondered how his mother was doing. Mary was an amazing soul and had just been through brain surgery to remove a tumor and a quadruple heart bypass before that. She always seemed to bounce back better than before. He worried about her of course, and he had been the one who had found her having fits in the bed before the ambulance came to take her to the hospital where they had found the tumor. He often remembered how she used to soothe him as a child when he had been wracked by those vivid dreams night after night. She would tuck him into bed and sing and pray to him with the Archangels, Auriel, Gabriel, Raphael, and Michael.

> *"Four Angels round my head*
> *Four angels at my bed*
> *One to watch and one to pray*
> *And two to guide my soul this day"*

She would surround him with warmth and tenderness so that in time the dreams would go away and he would be still and calm again in that blanket of love.

Altair decided to climb Cave Rock while he was waiting so he made his way upwards until there was only him, the world and sky with the ocean stretching all around him out to the horizon. Everything was painted blue and white with streaks of sunshine bouncing off the waves.

He stood in that stillness and silence for a long time before he made his way back down to the beach.

As he planted his feet on the sand he felt a grip on his arm and then another across his shoulders. He twisted this way and that to try to avoid the stranglehold getting tighter, but the grip wouldn't let go. He couldn't get his balance and then he felt a pressure on his left shoulder. The one he was so protective about. He had to alter his stance against Sam who was so much bigger. He could hear both their breathing, heavy and rushing fast, so he tensed, as if he was going to throw the heavier man, then he relaxed and went into a deep crouch and threw himself backwards. Sam fell back on the sand with Altair on top of him, but the grip did not ease one bit. He tugged and tried to roll backwards but then felt a sudden terrible weakness in his shoulder as with a sickening lurch the shoulder joint snapped out of its socket. Searing pain shot through his body like a lance had pierced his left side and he began to lose consciousness. Just as the last of his strength left him the most remarkable thing happened. Altair's vision was blurred and hazy and as he squeezed his eyes tight against the pain a hand of light reached out to him directly from the sky in his vision and a voice called,

"Son."

It was Sri Yukteswar.

He knew it without a doubt.

"Give me your hand."

Altair reached out to him and then lost consciousness.

Altair pitched off the side of the bridge and fell towards the river below. The battle surged on above. None of this mattered to Altair. The light was becoming transparent and the veil between him and the horror above was thinning. His heart felt like stone and his body was heavy.

Altair was no longer on the bridge, but he wasn't in the river either.

Altair turned towards the light and flew upwards, and reaching out felt a hand, the Elder, encouraging him onward.

It was the year 1959 and he was looking downwards on his next life, as a young man, born in the Deep South in 1961, a student of the Dalai Lama and Yogananda, writing a book which would change the world. He watched his path unfold, sharing portals of Presence through love, compassion, and wisdom. He saw himself as a much older man, with his mother Mary, in her final dying moments.

He was on 'night watch'.

"God bless you. I love you" he heard himself say. It was 4:06 am from the clock beside her bed. Her breathing was very shallow.

"You gave birth to me around this time so now you are going to rebirth yourself with the angels' help in God's Light and hold Dad's hand all the way back to heaven."

Then the breathing stopped.

"God bless you, Mum. I love you."

As Altair watched his older self in the Deep South take his mother Mary's hand a portal opened up in the room for all three of them.

Mary stepped into it the instant it opened.

The portal of radiant light.

They all knew many people described this sort of experience when they returned from a near-death experience. His little self from the Deep South had experienced this radiant light just after he was born as the doctors couldn't get him out of the birth canal, used forceps for delivery and had to revive him when the umbilical cord was wrapped tightly around his neck.

"The One True Self."

It was Mary's voice.

"Manifests briefly at the time of death in this portal of radiant light."

Altair and his self from the Deep South watched closely the same vision, aware that he would encounter the unmanifested timeless dimension in an experience with the Dalai Lama and the Kalachakra some years after his mother's passing. Letting go of fear and attachment to the senses and the material world is so important to passing through this portal they knew.

"Make your Presence strong enough in your life through meditation and prayer," said Mary, "and you will be strong enough for conscious immortality when you enter this portal of radiant light."

Then she was gone, on to other worlds to help and liberate others in just the same way as she had done with so much love for her Cambodian refugees in this one.

Altair still had hold of The Elder's hand.

"Who are you?"

"I am the One who shows you the way. You know how to use the portals?"

"Yes. Are you from this world? How do you know so much about me?"

"We all have a purpose much greater than we can ever imagine. That much I know about you. There is a war coming, greater than any war that has come before it, a battle between the forces of good and evil for balance, and you and so many others like you are playing your part in it. God made us, each of us, as a perfect image, and so God within us has the power to act and perform miracles as Christ Lights, Buddhas and Divine Mothers to defeat the powers of darkness and liberate this entire planet into the light. That is what the rest of the cosmos is waiting for. One entire collective consciousness to join in unity and speak as One in the light."

"I have always wanted that, dreamed of it, written about it, that we would all sing One Song."

"So, it is. That is why they named you the Singer who heals the Heart. That is why others recognize it in you, this power of unity consciousness, free of the restrictions of religion yet honoring all religions. You have it in you, the Light of the One Song. If you don't use it, the dark will wrest it from your grip and leave so many who would sing the same song with you wallowing in ignorance."

"Why me? Why not another?"

"It is time for us all to stand up and be counted. Could you not cast out the demon in Christ's name? Did you not receive guidance from Babaji and Krishna in the form of a scroll? Did you not receive a Chintamani Stone from the Heart of Avalokiteshvara Guan Yin?"

"Yes."

"Then say to others, 'You are a spiritual warrior. A being of love, compassion, and wisdom. A Christ Light. A Buddha within. A Divine Mother.' That is the message you come to bring to others. That they are the same as you. Very human and very divine."

Altair bowed low, seeing the power and the truth in those beautiful words. Knowing that as he embarked on his mission he would meet so many more on the same path with the same mission.

"Over all recorded time and then beyond that, the two great powers of good and evil have fought for supremacy through Earth Angels for the light and Agents of the dark. One teaches us love and compassion, wisdom and unity, while the other drags us down into fear, ignorance and separation. Each one of us has to choose, and the choice is about deep presence in the consciousness of one or the other, at any given moment. That is why the power of presence is so crucial. That is why mindfulness and heartfulness in the beginning of our path is so important to awaken us to what is right here and now."

"What do I do?"

"Ah, it is more important to be, then the doing flows quite naturally," smiled the Elder. "No matter how important other things may seem, like the busyness of this material world, trust in the flow, be still and know the Light of God within will guide your way. That light will always manifest someone to guide you as you have discovered, in human form like the Sanyasi, Messenger of Krishna, or in angelic form like Auriel."

Then they looked at each other. The Elder at Altair and Altair back at the Elder. And Altair saw Her for the first time, and those wise lines changed into the lines of ancient wisdom and those sharp eyes transformed into the eyes of the Lion of Bengal.

"Sri Yukteswar!" Tears flooded Altair's eyes in recognition. As the realization dawned on him, spreading over his face like the rising sun, Altair suddenly connected to his mother.

"You! You were the Elder who greeted my mother! You were the seed of wisdom that was planted from the very beginning!"

"I could never leave you, My Son. We always nurture the ones we love. Just like my most ardent disciple Yogananda. You and he are drawn to the same light. You have at heart the wisdom of the stars, just like me. You are a householder and will have a daughter just like me. Here I will show you your future."

The air was charged with the sounds of metal upon metal, cry meeting cry and feet pounding on turf. Wings and motors filled the air and poisonous vapors made Altair's stomach turn and the oceans and rivers surge in anger. He passed with Sri Yukteswar over centuries of human conflict, each lesson serving to teach mankind little about the inner conflict that was the true source of all such fear.

Suddenly they stopped in the middle of an enormous field.

Three men were waiting there for them. As they stood, four enormous armies emerged from hidden valleys on either side and either end and filled the land, the rivers, and the air.

"Varanasi, 2425, or more rightly put, Shambhala of the future," said Sri Yukteswar.

One of the other men spoke to Altair.

"You are the one I tasked with writing your diary, in the hope of many more yogis revealing themselves with their own diaries." He smiled, that beneficent smile that Altair knew so well.

"Master!" said Altair, falling to his knees, his eyes filled with tears. Waves of bliss engulfed him.

"We all have *siddhas* or powers," said Yogananda. "Our task on this earth is simple. To become aware of the daily battle between spirit and matter, soul and body, life and death, love and fear, wisdom and ignorance.

To bring freedom from fear through love, to liberate ignorance into wisdom, illuminate dark with light."

"Why don't you stop all this?"

The man next to Yogananda spoke.

"Even at Kurukshetra those blind to their sense illusions and ignorance would not listen to me. The power-mad do not accept a fair resolution and instead play out the battle of spirit and matter on this field of conflict, Varanasi."

"Lord Krishna!" Altair could see His glorious form, shimmering in the battle haze that was enveloping the field as the armies advanced.

The divine figure nodded in greeting and waved at the approaching forces.

"The message of the Bhagavad Gita is timeless. The armies around us symbolize the descent of the universe and people from spirit into matter. The Gita shows the process by which that descent may be reversed, enabling humanity to reascend from the limited consciousness of "I" and "me" as a mortal being to the immortal consciousness of the I AM Presence, the True Self, the soul, one with Infinite Spirit and God."

The last man spoke. As he gazed at Altair a beatific light shone from his eyes and struck Altair's heart. Before his astonished eyes, the battlefield transformed into transcendent splendor. Altair knew then with a thundering heart who he was standing in the presence of.

"Yes, it is I, Maitreya. As you can see all is not what it seems. The Kalachakra teaches us that the great battle fought here in 2425 is really the inner battle against samsara. These armies, as Lord Krishna said, represent our misguided passion, aggression, and ignorance. Those are the forces of the dark. The forces of the light, the four armies of Shambhala, represent the antidote of the inner poisons, the four immeasurables, love, compassion, joy, and equanimity, and in the final battle the defeat of the leader of the dark hordes is the defeat of fear itself."

"The Bible and the Yoga of Jesus, the Bhagavad Gita, and the Vajrayana teachings of the Kalachakra all show the yogi how this process unfolds within the body," said Yogananda.

"The Yoga of Jesus," said Altair, "Christ, Krishna, Buddha and Divine Mother."

"The perfect unity of their revelations," said Yogananda, "is revealed when studied carefully and meditated upon with soul-awakened intuitive perception."

"A universal consciousness," said Altair.

"That Universal Consciousness," said Yogananda, "the Kutastha Chaitanya, Buddhahood or Krishna Consciousness, which we also call Christ, was fully manifested in the incarnation of Jesus, Buddha, Krishna and all Divine Mothers and it can also be manifested in your consciousness."

"A Christ Light," said Sri Yukteswar, "is a person who frees their soul from the consciousness of the body and unites it with the Christ Consciousness that pervades all of creation."

"The consciousness of love, compassion, and wisdom," said Altair.

Epilogue

Yogananda's words carried the vibration of a portal of presence. As he spoke to Altair a great Light descended on the fields of Shambhala.

"Come with me," said the Light. "Fear grows in the hearts of men and women. You know your mission, to bring freedom from fear through love. Follow me."

Altair left the field of battle and did not look back.

From far off in the valleys and hills, Altair could make out a village approaching as he followed the Light. He saw a stream running just behind the village and a cave above, and just beyond that a young man and woman were seated at the entrance, in deep meditation.

Altair came to the cave entrance and bowed.

The young man and woman opened their eyes and raised their gaze to meet Altair's. He knew them both immediately. The Avatars Babaji and Mataji. He saw that between them there lay a bundle tightly wrapped in swaddling clothes. He bowed low again.

"This is your daughter," said Babaji.

"She will come to you and Padma when the time is right," said Mataji.

"Her name is Maia," said Babaji. "Brave Warrior Princess of the Light."

"Keep her safe until it is time for her to seek her fortune and discover the Christ Consciousness within Her and share that Light with all people."

"So be it," said Altair.

And so, it was.

Then Altair was gone, following the Light.

"That is the real miracle," said Babaji to Mataji at the entrance of the cave.

"All little children on earth are Christ Lights when they are born."

"All earth needs is for enlightened parents and teachers to remind children who they really are, with the care and affection of divine mothers," said Mataji.

Free Extract from 'Diary of A Yogi Guide – Portals of Presence'

Introduction

'Diary of a Yogi' is based on a simple universal principle.

That as we develop deep silence and stillness, and touch the Divine Presence within us, we can sense the One Shared Heart in all creatures, the consciousness that is one with our own.

We learn how to love everything as ourselves, to love our neighbour as ourselves, to see past the outer form and know the inner essence which is timeless, nameless and formless.

Once we see all beings as ourselves, we realize we can communicate with all things across time and space, whether they be Jesus or Buddha, star beings or starcraft, dolphins or snakes, Chintamani Stones and pearls, the rose and the lotus.

Like all portals of presence, words contemplated deeply create shifts within us, and this book's main purpose is to create a shift in consciousness, to awaken us. That is why I say that all who read 'Diary of a Yogi' are awakeners. Like the Chintamani Stone, the lotus flower, the phoenix and the dragon, which are all portals of presence, making us more transparent to the light of consciousness within us, an inner transformation that is radical and profound is the state of consciousness of an awakener. As you shift, others around you feel the shift, and awaken spiritually too.

When we are alert, still and silent and present with the words, when we contemplate them deeply in our heart, our own divine life essence, the consciousness that exists in every being, awakens from its sleep, and love blossoms. We see that same divine consciousness in all living things and we love it as our own, as one, as the shared heart.

Chapter 1, Samye, is about the vibration of dreams. When we have dreams, and contemplate them deeply, certain dreams resonate with us as signs, becoming like the words in a book, portals that create shifts within us. Dreams are the first portal of presence in the book 'Diary of a Yogi – A Book of Awakening.'

The sign Altair was given as a child, was a dream, a dream of a Tibetan monk, on the bridge of Samye Monastery, and it provided him with a portal of deep contemplation into the nature of birth, death and the interconnection of all life, and life beyond life.

For Altair's mother Mary, a Maori Elder guided Mary into knowledge and wisdom that the source wanted Mary to have about this dream, to pass it on to her son, to help him to accomplish his mission here on earth.

Chapter 2, Zahor, is about the vibration of visions. When we have visions, certain visions resonate with us as signs, that when contemplated deeply create shifts in us, awakening us to the consciousness we share with all living things, including the deities or other manifestations that arise in the visions. Visions are the second portal of presence in the book 'Diary of a Yogi.'

The visions and dreams Altair wrote about are only to give you inspiration to follow your own visions and dreams as signs of portals for deeper contemplation into awakening.

The vision at Zahor was a sign for Altair that the wisdom of Padmasambhava, Yeshe Tsogyal and Princess Mandarava, was a spiritual teaching that would benefit his awakening, once contemplated deeply.

We all receive visions that are signs of awakening like this at different times in our lives.

Visions come in the form of the light and also can come in the guise of darkness, beckoning us to transform into light, to help the light of consciousness within us arise. We are that light.

Trust your heart and your path to lead you into the light.

The suffering of the human heart and the light and darkness of the spiritual path are all necessary to dissolve the ego that is the main barrier to the light of consciousness awakening. Yet all are necessary, the suffering, the light, the darkness, and the ego, to awaken.

Every one of you is unique and no one path is identical to another's.

Some of you, through life's circumstances, being naturally very positive and light, use the light to radiate more light, and reach balance.

> "If your eye is single, then your whole body is full of light." (Matthew 6:22)

Some of you, through life's circumstances, may be very negative and heavy, and use the darkness to transform into light and reach balance.

> "The people who walked in darkness have seen a great light." (Isaiah 9:2)

Great saints and yogis suffer from feelings of isolation, abandonment, depression, fear, and loss. St Ignatius, whose spiritual exercises I practiced as a child, spoke of the desolation and turmoil he felt in God's absence. Yogananda plunged into two years of depression at his mother's death. We all touch times in our lives when we feel light and other times in our life when we feel darkness.

All ways lead home and all paths are by nature One.

That is the way of the source.

Portals of Presence – Samye – Dream Yoga

As a tiny baby we enter the world with innocence as Christ Lights, filled with the joy of being, and peace at heart. There is a radiance that comes with babies that is not of this world and we all recognize it. As children of God or source, as awakened Buddhas, we have a Chintamani Stone within us, a priceless jewel of wisdom, a wish-fulfilling treasure, that we look to the world and grown-ups to provide us with guidance in how to nurture and use it.

We naturally feel oneness with God or love at source. When we connect deeply in later life through true love or profound natural or spiritual experiences, the whole world suddenly takes on a new vibrant hue and we touch our true nature within, the divine light of consciousness, which is nameless, timeless, and formless and helps us see beyond the veil of appearances that preoccupies our senses most of the time.

If we focus too much on the external material world throughout our lives we begin to perceive we are separate and develop fear and attachment as we try to hang on to the many things we think are outside of ourselves, and we lose that divine innocence and the power of presence in being.

We lose the knowing that we are the light.

My first perception of the world was through a dream of a consciousness, one that existed in the past, as a monk at Samye Monastery in 1959. That dream, an experience I had every night over the period of a year from when I was two years old until when I was three, awoke a deep desire in me to know how and where that consciousness came from, what it was and what it was trying to inform me of. I was divinely curious, one might say, at a very early age, about my mission and purpose in life, one I saw as being interwoven with magic and the stars.

When we are young our mind is very innocent and pure, like clay that has not been sculpted and lies still, in the form of a precious Buddha, Christ or Divine Mother. This power of divine being that lies within from such an early age cannot be found by grasping or searching for it, paradoxically, as that is like using the Buddha to search for the Buddha. It can only be found when the mind is clear, pure, and still. Like a tranquil lake. When you look across a still lake on an early morning you can feel the presence I am speaking of. The sacred realm, the vast infiniteness of being is accessible to us all, at any point in our life. I became curious why the entire world was not involved in a collective desire for awakening, unity, and peace. I wondered how we could best establish presence and knowledge of I AM, the awareness that comes before thinking I am this, or I am that, and I do this, or I own that.

The deeper 'I'.

I naturally began with dreams and the yoga of dreams. For me, this was exploring and contemplating the true nature of dreams as a portal of presence and how to be present in the dream experience. I wondered how I could use the same presence I felt as a child, that I was consciously developing when I was awake, while I was asleep. Dreams seemed an ideal portal to explore that. A portal of presence.

We are constantly thinking. As the saying goes, we have 60,000 thoughts a day, 40,000 of them which we had yesterday. Unless we are well trained in mindful and heartful practice, 80% of those thoughts will be negative. "I can't do this" or "I'm not such and such" are very common reflections on life.

The incessant mental thoughts make the internal world we live in very noisy.

Try it now. Let your mind grow calm and take your attention and awareness to your breathing.

"Breathing in" as you breathe in.

"Breathing out" as you breathe out.

Notice the silence and stillness and presence that follows as you contemplate the breath.

This is the light of consciousness arising within you.

As you breathe for longer periods, thoughts will come. Pay attention to your breathing and notice where your mind goes. Does it stay on the breath or does it wander into thoughts, sounds, and distractions like the past and future?

Does it surrender and reach deeper into the silence and stillness?

When thoughts come, see them like waves on the ocean.

Notice when a wave comes, when you are distracted. Label the distraction. If you notice a sound, label it "sound" and if you feel an ache or pain arising in the body notice it, "knee ache". If you find yourself thinking about the past, name it "past" or "family" if you have been concerned about a family member and if your thoughts wander into the future label it "future" or "job" if you worried about the plans you need to have in place for tomorrow's schedule in your job.

Make friends with your thoughts, get to know them, their habits and routines. This is the awakening of awareness. Naming your thoughts has a special magic, takes away their power and releases their energy and consciousness back to you, taking you one step closer to the nameless realm of being.

The world of thoughts and thinking is filled with problems and conflicts, a long way away from the realm of divine innocence and joy we knew as an infant in the arms of our mother. That is what we are returning to, with new awareness and wisdom, an inner world filled with love and care and affection like a Divine Mother.

The Divine Mother who knows how to take care of us is deep inside and has always been there. She is our true self.

When we enter the world of sleep and dreams we are given a unique opportunity to nurture and care for ourselves through the power of dream sleep and dreamless sleep. Dreams bring a message that can be very useful in interpreting and making sense of what is occurring in our subconscious mind. Dreams may also be useful in going beyond that into more subtle awareness such as prophecy, insight into the past, past consciousness and understanding the future and what it has in store for us. If we stay conscious in the dreaming process this is called lucid dreaming where we know we are dreaming. Beyond that is the state of dreamless sleep, where we merge with source and lose all sense of I am this or that and draw upon vital energies to rejuvenate. There is no longer a "me". With practice our dreams and our dreamless sleep will be timeless, nurturing, restful and at peace, at one with all things.

Much of what I write here is spontaneous, drawn out from within in response to questions from many of you. I see these dialogues as discussions of the shared heart in that the wisdom is as much the questioner's as the one who answers. We all speak from Oneness when deeply in presence, interconnected and in true relationship.

Here is one such dialogue.

"I often find the meaning of renunciation hard to grasp. Can you elaborate on inner renunciation? Is it surrender?"

Inner renunciation.
It is a very subtle process of surrender.
Let me try to elaborate because I think it is crucial to enlightenment, the end of all suffering.

Most people understand renunciation in terms of giving up something, addictions perhaps, like food, alcohol or sex, or whatever they know they are attached to, sense addictions.

Those are important and are easy to identify.

As long as you are 'busy' in terms of 'the material world' you find that your mind and consciousness is 'pulled out' as it were, so it is difficult to even begin to perceive the vastness of the inner world because you are rarely aware of it.

Inner renunciation is much deeper and requires considerable mastery, meaning time and practice.

To begin, the most essential practice is mindfulness, which both the Buddha, in the Anapanasati Sutra and Mary Magdalene in the Gospel of St Mary mention.

"Mindfulness of breath," as the Buddha says,

and "Where your mind is, there lies the treasure" as Mary Magdalene says.

The first key is awareness of what you are connecting to, and therefore in an inner way what you are attached to or addicted to.

These are the sense thoughts rather than the sense objects.

Much subtler to perceive.

Many people are not aware of their thoughts and therefore find the prospect of witnessing them challenging,

This is why mindfulness of the breath is so important.

In being mindful of, for example, "breathing in, I am aware I am breathing in" now opens a whole new world.

Because you suddenly become aware of just how difficult it is for the mind to do this, and how often it gets distracted.

Or attached.

How addicted it is to 'movement'.

Now the seeker understands the importance of Psalm 46:10 "Be still and know God".

Setting time aside for stillness and silence is actually to open the portal to God.

Once awareness develops.

The mind which in its pure state is the Buddha begins to become aware of itself and its attachments.

The true self becomes aware of the "me" with all its anxiety, attachments and neuroses.

It starts the process of letting go or surrendering, through mindful and heartfulness practice.

Self-compassion.

Awakening.

Giving time to let go or learning how to surrender those thoughts and emotions that block us from perceiving God within.

That compassion eventually brings wisdom.

The wisdom learned naturally directs more compassion towards the human condition in yourself and others, which is the path of the Bodhisattva, liberator or awakener.

Every time you help someone to free themselves of an anxious thought they have been struggling with, the path towards their own Buddhahood within gets clearer.

The mind creates a screen, like a movie superimposed over reality, that is filled with names and images, words and concepts that are not the true picture. They are our perspective, much the same way as in the famous story of the blind men and the elephant. The blind men each touch a part of the elephant like her trunk or her tail and then describe the elephant based on this limited perspective. We are like that, projecting our partial experience of reality as the whole truth. This partial perspective is the veil that hinders us in having true relationships with others, that blocks us from interconnectedness, that creates separation between us and the sacred, with source, God, love. This is the movie screen of our thoughts that creates the illusion of separateness and creates a "me" and an "I" that does this and that. We divorce ourselves from the innocent divine self and no longer even feel this Oneness with source but instead fall into the pit of conflict, divided thoughts and eventually despair.

The dream experience itself can be highly illuminating when seen as a practice, like dream yoga. When we awake from our dreams we know we have been dreaming, and when we awake from this illusion of "I" and "me" we begin to see the many beliefs we have about life are also like dreaming. They are merely perspectives, dreams, until we make them realities through our own experience, which then have the power to liberate us.

Practice

Here is a simple dream yoga technique to try.

The same presence you are practicing during your waking hours, being mindful of the breath, try applying to your sleeping hours.
    Before you go to sleep, meditate using some of the meditation practices I have on the website or SoundCloud or your own practice or Yogananda's handbook on Kriya Yoga that is available. Try doing at least 10 minutes a night.
    As you go to sleep use the conscious breath or being mindful of your breathing to help you fall asleep.
    Keep a dream journal beside your bed so you can note anything that occurs if you wake immediately following a dream,
    If you wake, note down the dream and return to mindful breathing to put you back to sleep.
    Practice conscious presence during dreams.
    Contemplate how deep your dreams become and how close to the deeper "I", the divine presence in dreaming, they are.

Here is a more advanced practice from Tibetan Buddhism

Work with the vital energies through Kriya Yoga as outlined by Yogananda and Babaji while you are awake. Gather the vital energies into the central channel, dissolve them and allow the experience of the clear light of being to enter. Then when dreams occur recognize them as dreams.

If this proves challenging, cultivate a strong resolution to retain conscious awareness in the dream state. When meditating, meditate on the throat chakra especially.

Even if you are not trained you can sometimes experience a clear dream and retain awareness in it. If you concentrate strongly on a particular activity all day you may often dream of it at night and be aware of the dream.

For example, it is most useful to meditate upon yourself as the mandala deity, so as the Christ or Guan Yin or any other deity you are attuned to as your Self and meditate also upon the guru within and practice devotion to him or her. Offer prayers that you may experience many dreams, that your dreams be clear and auspicious, and that you retain awareness in your dreams. You can practice using the mantra syllable OM and visualize it inside the central channel at the center of the throat chakra and hold awareness on that spot.

In addition, you can try transformative exercises such as consciously initiating a dream pattern or transforming the dream altogether. You can project yourself on the rays of the sun or the moon to a celestial realm or to a faraway human realm and see what is there.

Another practice involves beyond-the-world dreams where you consciously project yourself in the dream to star fields or through star gates such as Sirius or the Pleiades, through Christ Grids from sacred spaces on the earth such as the capstone of the Great Pyramid at Giza, or into various buddhafields such as Sukhavati, Tushita, and Akanishta where you can meet the buddhas and bodhisattvas and listen to them and receive their teachings, activations, and initiations. You can practice this during the day so that when it arrives in your dream at night you can be that much more aware and present.

Please note that the pure realms experienced in the initial stages of this practice are just reflections of the real realm. It is not that easy to experience the actual pure dimensions. Your consciousness must be molded and shaped by your practice to be of the same purity.

Prophecies received of future happenings may be true and the same applies to dream visions of past lives. You should apply yogic techniques for increasing reliability such as can you repeat the experience several times and experience it and transform it if you wish and can you meditate in the dream and retain presence and experience the clear light of being.

(Inspired with deepest gratitude by the Six Yogas of Naropa.)

We are all exploring consciousness, existence, and bliss together in the One Shared Heart. The dialogues we have here and the experiences we share are all important to our awakening so please share your dreams as you experience them on my website if you feel guided to, and I will too. I will do my best to answer all questions you have on the website either individually or when the numbers are too great by a group response.

Love and soul blessings
Altair

CPSIA information can be obtained
at www.ICGtesting.com
Printed in the USA
LVHW090731280121
677609LV00005B/450